Paula Ann McDonald's story will grip your heart, grieve your soul and give you hope for the most abused people you can imagine. If it were not for my having met with the county sheriff and county attorney involved, I would have a hard time believing such a bizarre and abusive family existed in the U.S. today. And if it were not for knowing Paula personally, I would have a hard time believing anyone could come out of such a nightmare and be transformed into a beautiful instrument for God's healing grace. If you think you've got it tough, read Paula's story. If you don't believe there is life-transforming hope for those having suffered years of horrible abuse, read Paula's story. As someone who directs a ministry to victims of child sex trafficking, I believe your hope will be renewed, as has mine.

—Jerry Peyton
Director, Streetlight Tucson
A Ministry of the Crisis Pregnancy Centers of Tucson

From My Father's Hands
To My
Father's Hands

PAULA ANN MCDONALD

WestBow
PRESS
A DIVISION OF THOMAS NELSON

Scripture taken from the New King James Version. Copyright 1979, 1980, 1982 by Thomas Nelson, inc. Used by permission. All rights reserved.

WestBow Press books may be ordered through booksellers or by contacting:

WestBow Press
A Division of Thomas Nelson
1663 Liberty Drive
Bloomington, IN 47403
www.westbowpress.com
1-(866) 928-1240

ISBN: 978-1-4497-3785-6 (e)
ISBN: 978-1-4497-3784-9 (sc)
ISBN: 978-1-4497-3783-2 (hc)

Library of Congress Control Number: 2012901271

Printed in the United States of America

WestBow Press rev. date: 02/29/2012

Acknowledgments

To the many, many "hands and feet of Jesus," who have helped me along this very painful, and yet wonderful, journey!

First to my sister, Ellie, without whom I'm sure I could not have endured at times.

To Dennis and Teresa Tagas; Suzann and Larry Arvila (my adoptive mom and dad); Bob and Gayanne Waller. (Bob, I know you watch from the great view you have in the heavens!) To Ginger Fisher, who stuck by me through thick and thin, and also took my terrible scribble and put it into the computer; and to Shawna Hansen for going through my manuscript, editing, and giving me all your encouragement!

To my church family in Payson Arizona; Randy and Kathy Kaufman; Steve and Judy Perham; and to our wonderful pastors, who I'm sure wondered, at times, if there was hope. To Curt and Wendy Mattson, Steve and Carmen Cook, Jerry and Georgia Peyton, and many more—you know who you are: Thank you more than words can say; you loved me into healing.

To my wonderful husband and his family, and last but not least, to our wonderful children, what a blessing you all are! I'm so blessed! May God bless you. I will never forget all the love and support!

Contents

Preface

As I write the story of my childhood, I understand that there are many who have suffered as children. However, the purpose of telling my story is to build a rapport with those in need and, most importantly, to tell my story of wonderful redemption; this is the only reason I have written about these very painful abuses.

I pray that the message of redemption comes through stronger than any other, as the pain of rejection and fear I endured will never measure up to the healing I have received or the hope I have of spending eternity with my Lord and Savior.

My hope is to help each and every hurting person who reads this see that they, too, can "Come to Me, all *you* who labor and are heavy laden, and I will give you rest. Take My yoke upon you and learn from Me, for I am gentle and lowly in heart, and you will find rest for your souls. For My yoke *is* easy and My burden is light." (Matthew 11:28–30 NKJV). This is a promise from Jesus!

It is so important to know deep down inside how much you are loved by your heavenly Father. I am living proof.

Many names have been changed to protect the innocent and not so innocent.

Chapter 1
Ladybugs

THE MORNING IS SO PEACEFUL; I breathe in deeply and look around me at the small but beautiful back yard my husband and I have designed together. I'm enjoying the peace and quiet of my life. It is a little lonely with all the kids grown and gone, but I have promised myself I will start to do some of the things I never had a chance to do.

My mind continues to wonder, what will I do? I've never had an opportunity to make these kinds of choices. But then as my often cruel past starts to flood my memories I'm not sure I want to remember.

However, life today is so good, how could I have ever lived through those days? Is it just a bad dream? I quickly know it was never a dream since the memories are still so real.

My mind starts down the road remembering the cruelty, abuse, I remember the cries of my brothers and sisters, I remember the pain, fear, confusion and rejection of my own life, the abuse of every kind. I don't want to remember it, I want to stay in today with the peace and beauty of my present life!

Then I remember how many times I've been encouraged to tell my story of heart sickening abuse, and my beautiful story of redemption, and I know I must remember and write. I'm ready, but where did all the craziness start? I let my mind wonder back, way back......

Look at all of the tumbleweeds and trees—very big trees. What a wonderful world! I couldn't take it all in, and it seemed quite overwhelming. It was very warm, and everything was very dry. I just wanted to keep looking.

I don't remember the drive to our new home in the very small settlement twenty miles from the city. When I arrived it seemed very exciting to me, and then I heard my little sister say, "Look at all the ladybugs." Sure enough, as would happen many times in our childhood, Ellie would show me what she had caught. I decided to do the same.

For hours, we caught ladybugs and were amazed at how they just seemed to disappear from our hands. We would think we had caught one, but when we opened our hands, it would be gone. I guess we had holes in our hands! At that time, I didn't know just how important all of the animals and other critters were going to be to me as I grew up in the valley.

The valley was scary in many ways. One of these ways was when we were told, "Girls, be careful out there; there are rattlesnakes." We would soon learn what rattlesnakes looked like. That first summer we were there, many were killed. I only have a few memories of that summer because I was only three going on four years old.

My sister and I were only eleven and a half months apart, and we never celebrated a birthday separately until I married. Ellie and I did everything together. I'm sure there were many things that occurred that summer that my older brothers and sisters can remember, but this was my main memory.

Chapter 2
The Snake

AS I SAID, SNAKES WERE A REAL PROBLEM. They seemed to be everywhere, and you could never be too careful. One night, after working all day, three of my older brothers, Ellie, and I were playing outside just as it was getting dark. Ellie and one of the brothers heard a noise, and it sounded like a cicada. (This is an insect that starts out as a bug and lives in the ground until it is mature and then comes to the surface, crawls up an object, and hatches. It then is able to fly and also makes a strange noise that could be mistaken. Ellie thought there was one by a cinderblock, and my older brother said, "Well, get it." However, when Ellie reached down to get it, she was bitten by a baby rattlesnake.

I was far too young to understand how serious this was, and even though my dad was very upset, he seemed to think that he could handle it on his own. I remember him putting the small cut in her finger at the site of the bite in his mouth and sucking very hard on her finger. Then her hand was soaked in disinfectant. I remember feeling scared just because there was so much obvious fear with the older ones, but I really couldn't understand.

Ellie's hand and arm swelled all the way up to her neck. I don't remember how long it took for her to heal, but as I grew older, I realized how serious this situation really was and that my sister should have received medical help.

My father's arrogance only grew from there! It was as if he felt that if he just prayed and did whatever he thought was right at the time, then he didn't need a doctor or anyone else, such as pastors. I thank God that my sister lived, and it is him I give the credit to. He was merciful, as he knew that he had great things for my sister to do.

Chapter 3
New Job

"I'LL GIVE YOU A PIECE OF GUM if you watch cows for a little while," Tom, one of my older brothers, said. I don't remember ever hesitating; for a piece of gum, I would do pretty much anything. It was that old fashioned bubblegum. I never got the gum right at that moment, and most of the time never did, but the very thought of getting it was enough for me. More often than not, the thought was all I got. Tom rarely came through with his promises. I guess the training began there for me in many ways.

Ellie and I started watching the cows, actually heifers, three of them, pregnant, in the spring or summer when I was four. At first, it was just a few times a week for a few hours, then it became sunup to sundown, day in and day out. We would get up at the break of dawn and take the cows out. Then, when it was breakfast time, we would take turns watching the cows as the other one ate.

During certain times of the year, the weeds along the side of the road were very high. These weeds were the food for the cattle. Among the weeds were mesquite trees, wonderful wild sunflowers, gourds, four–o'clocks, and other wildflowers. I found a bit of joy in all of this at first, even though the hours were long.

Both my sister and I would grow to love the cattle, and when the first three calves were born, all bulls, we then had to care for them.

Each of the cows had her own personality, and even though they had horns, we were able to grow very close to one of them, Smokey, who was named for the hot breath she would breathe when it was cold. It came out in large clouds, more so than with any of the other cows. Smokey would let us get close when it was cold. We would put our hands on her udder when it was really cold to keep them from freezing. Smokey never seemed to mind it much. My sister and I were not dressed very warmly for winter, and I can remember begging to go in the house, but unless it was raining or snowing, we had to stay outside until dark.

Smokey let us milk her as time went on, and we did drink her milk even though goat milk was the primary milk used at home. Smokey would do crazy things, such as lay too close to the fence and roll under it while sleeping, ending up on the wrong side when she woke up. She was very willing to give us a hassle if we wanted her to hurry up. She always lagged behind, and if she ate a gourd, there was no getting her to turn loose. We would put our hands as far as we could down her throat to pull it back, even getting caught in the "cud chewing teeth" at the back to get it. Why, one might ask? Well, if gourds get started in a field, they are very destructive and very hard to get rid of. Gourds will take over a field, and the only way to get rid of them is with herbicides and lots of hard work. But that being said, one may still ask why.

Well, things started to change rapidly for my sister and I as consequences became more severe. We tried harder and harder to keep out of trouble, and if a cow or a bull ate a gourd, the seeds came out whole with their own fertilizer. When my dad became aware that they were growing in the fields, the punishment was a spanking, along with yelling and accusations of how lazy and stupid and useless we were. Oh, it hurt, so we tried very hard not to upset our dad.

Licker, named for always licking us on our shoes, hands, faces, etc., was larger than the other cows and very beautiful. She also gave us the best-looking calves, always bulls. Her horns were straight out, and they could easily have hurt us. She was quite sassy at times, but predictable. I always respected her with a tad bit of fear.

The first year that she calved, she had a beautiful bull calf and we saved him for breeding purposes. We named him Red Bull, and he would grow up to be a very beautiful, healthy, and gentle bull.

Gentle and *bull* are usually words not put together, but he was exceptional and my sister and I would grow to love this bull. We rode him and he never tried to hurt us. However, when he got tired of us on his back he would simply head for a mesquite tree and scrape us off, although we learned to jump off before he arrived at the tree. We would have Red Bull nine years, and I could write a book on him alone. Such a gentle giant, he weighed about eighteen hundred pounds.

There were times that he did scare my sister and me: when he would see the neighbor's bull that was a huge Black Angus. The only thing between them was a barbed wire fence and either one or two small girls yelling and hitting him with a stick if we could find one soon enough, or our bare hands, all the while yelling, "Red Bull, get away!" The dirt would be flying as he dug it up and threw it over his back, ready to charge the bull on the other side. The bull on the other side was doing the same thing. It was scary then, but as I look back, I wonder how my dad could have put two small girls in such a dangerous position.

There were times when people drove up or down our road, taking pictures and pointing at us as we worked, controlling the large animals that only older people should have been caring for.

"Tuffy," named for her stubborn ways, was a somewhat sad looking cow and I always felt rather sorry for her, but also a little afraid of her. She tossed her head a lot and was skittish. She seemed colder than the other cows and her calves were never as nice looking.

Each year, three calves were born and, if they were bulls, they were left uncastrated until they were butchered, That made them more aggressive as they grew older, but I remember that it was fun to try to ride them as soon as they were big enough, and my sister and I did.

We did crazy things with those cattle, but they were our lives. Even though we rode them, they were not as gentle as Red Bull, and so we had to hang on really well. Sometimes they fought when we were on them, and we worked at hanging on as long as we could—what fun! We were stepped on many times.

My sister was much tougher than I was in everything. She was fearless: fearless of the animals, the dark, and our brothers. I was not. I always struggled with fear. My fear ran away with me, and many things reinforced it as time went on. Ellie was the one who always said, "Come on, hurry up, just do it." We both had knees that never healed from one time to the next from that road. Many times, we fell as we tried to keep up with the cattle.

About once or twice a month they would decide to stampede, and even though the highest count I think was nine, when that many start running it is very hard to stop them. We learned the signs: a tail twitch, a head throw, and if we didn't run up to that cow or calf and tell it, "No!" in our strongest voice—and that often didn't help—away it would go, with all the rest after it. There were times that they would run a mile with us running as fast as we could; we would be crying and screaming, "Stop!" and trying to get in front and stop them.

Don't ask me why the cattle usually did listen to us; a stick or a slap with the hand usually made them stop, but not when they stampeded. It was the the worst, and often it happened when my sister or I was alone.

Summer and winter brought some very hard times. Getting up on a cold winter morning, the temperature was often freezing. I can still remember trying to find clothes that would help me stay warm. Where are the girls? Are the cows out yet? Those were daily questions from the age of four to the age of about eleven. Afterward, though I would still tend the cattle, it was less often as I was needed more in the house, and it was determined that my sister could care for the cows alone.

Wintertime came with cold and less feed for the cattle. The dry grass that was left over from the summer was not nearly as filling, so even though we were often very cold, we had to stay out there so the cattle could feed as long as possible.

My sister and I had really trained the cattle, though, and if we could get the cattle about half a mile or so from our house around noon each day, the cattle would want to lay down for a spell and nap. On a cold clear winter day with the wind blowing, as it always did during winter in the valley, there was nothing that two tired and cold little girls would enjoy more than to sneak a little nap with the cattle.

Smokey was our favorite to snuggle up to, and we put our hands just between a back leg and her udder. She would actually let us stay there, and many times, I'm sure I slept for at least thirty minutes. The cold made me so tired, as did the stress of our home that seemed to grow every day; I needed to nap. Some days it was the only peace I found; however, whenever a family member caught us, we were sure to pay. The nap would be reported to my dad and my stomach would tighten, as I would say, "Yes, I let the cattle lie down."

I'm not sure if my dad ever knew that my sister and I sometimes fell asleep, or that our purpose in having the cattle lie down to nap was to warm up in the winter or get out of the heat in the summer and, if possible, nap. (Cattle do need to take a break and chew their cuds to move food from one stomach to another.)

My sister and I had figured out a great way of getting the cattle to lie down. We simply kept them from leaving a small circle until one cow would lie down, then another, then they would all lie down. It took time to teach them this, but when you are desperate, you just figure things out. As the old saying goes, "necessity is the mother of invention," and I lived a large part of my life based on that, as survival was a large part of growing up for me.

Spring was always welcomed and brought more food for the cattle and the promise of calves. This was always exciting; seeing the cattle have plenty of food always gave us a good feeling. We loved to see the cows' bellies full and round.

There are two times that stand out in my mind far more than any others, in terms of very scary and sad times when taking care of the cattle. One was when my sister stepped on a nail. We didn't like to tell our parents when something was wrong for fear of getting into trouble. It always seemed to be our fault when we were hurt.

This time, however, I was the one who kept begging my sister to wait just one more day to tell. I wanted her company, and of course her help, so badly that I put her life in danger. One day, about four or five days after she had stepped on the nail, we looked at the wound; she had a huge knot that was full of pus with a red streak about six inches up her leg. To any other family that might mean a trip to the doctor, but to ours that meant that you had to soak your foot in a disinfectant. Then the sore was cut open and squeezed. There was no pain medicine; we were just told, "Shut up, it was your fault anyway".

My sister could not tend cattle for several days because she had to soak her foot until the red streak was gone. I truly felt guilty as I watched her. My stepmother would work on her foot and tell her not to scream and to just deal with it. Tough times like those occurred quite often. We were never allowed to scream, not even from extreme pain.

The other time that was very sad—and I still feel sick when I think about it—was when my sister and I were wanting to bring the cows in a little earlier, as it was one of those rare times that we had company.

My aunt was there and we were delighted just to see any family, as that really only happened maybe once a year. We enjoyed the evening, but during the night, the cattle broke out and got into the cornfield, ruining a large area. The rage in my father could not be matched as he yelled at us, whipping us both with the hose that he used: a piece of black PVC pipe that was always ready and waiting on the hood of the stove in the kitchen

For the rest of our punishment, we had to go out into our new alfalfa field, that in the beginning had more weeds than alfalfa, and pull weeds. We were to pull weeds, and there had better be load after load after wheelbarrow load coming out of that field. We pulled weeds all day, and by three that afternoon there was a huge pile of green, fresh weeds. All of the cattle and goats had eaten all day on that pile.

Soon one goat after another began to cry out and fall on the ground. We wondered what could be wrong with the goats. Scared, we ran to our older brother who confirmed that the goats were bloating from eating too many fresh weeds too fast. My dad was livid. We were ordered to run the goats and cattle to work off some of the feed. We ran them until we thought we were going to die.

Dad determined that the goats were too close to death and should be killed. Because it was so warm and flies were a problem, my brothers worked feverishly to get nine of the goats butchered and into the freezer.

My father's anger was aimed at me, and whenever he walked by he would hit me; it didn't matter where, he would just hit me. I was so sad and scared, for both my sister and myself, as well as for the animals. My father was angry for several days. The rejection, anger, and fear I felt made me wish I were dead. The first night I slept in the barn in the hay because I was too scared to go into the house. My brothers had already been thrown out and had slept in the barn for most of the year.

I had realized, by this time in my life, that I had some very severe problems, and I often cried myself to sleep asking Jesus for help. To the outside world, we appeared to be a very religious family. We thought we were religious also, but in truth, Satan had reign in our family.

Chapter 4
No Mom

I'M NOT SURE WHEN IT REALLY BECAME CLEAR TO ME that I was missing my mom; she had died when my sister was eleven and a half months old, and I was almost two. There has always been speculation that my mother didn't actually die from kidney stones.

My mom was forty-two, and five months pregnant, when she passed away. My dad didn't believe in contraception. Dad always talked religiously and used guilt through religion to get what he wanted. My mother had three children from a previous marriage, and all of them feel that there was foul play involved with our mother's death. As a small girl, I really didn't know what it meant that my mother was dead, but I did feel a deep loneliness that I later understood to be the void left by not knowing my mother and not having her teach and protect and love me.

I guess the reality, conscious or unconscious, began to settle in when I was around five years old, when the first of thirteen younger half siblings was born in 1970. It's not so much that I was ignored, but that I watched as my stepmom, eighteen years younger than my dad, loved and cared for this new half-sister with such attention and protective love that I had never been given even before this new sister was born.

In 1970 our family consisted of three stepchildren (my mother's from a previous marriage; none of these children lived with us on a regular basis), my father's six children (from a previous marriage), and my sister and I from our mother (who had passed away in 1967). Now my father was remarried and our first new half sister was born.

I'm not sure, but this may be where life really started to change for me. There was so much; even now as I write, it all comes flooding back to me and I have to write so fast just to keep memories from getting lost in the shuffle.

My dad made custom counter tops and worked very long hours. I started school and my older brothers and sisters were causing problems. There also was pain and sadness at the loss of my mother. The older children often told me about how wonderful she was! She loved us all and was a wonderful, kind, loving woman who always wanted to care for and protect children.

She had shown the older children just what a truly loving mom was, and she helped, in the four short years she was in their lives, to show them the love of Jesus. Then with the marriage of Dad and the babysitter, also known as our new stepmom, eighteen years old-eighteen years younger than my dad (and the same age as Dad's oldest daughter), it was war from day one. I started to feel the real effects after the first girl was born.

Every day was exhausting. By the time I was 6 and my sister Ellie 5 we had the care of the cattle after school until dark, a late supper, and then had dishes to clean for at least ten people. Not only did things deteriorate for our family, but also I became more aware as I grew older and understood more. My dad worked long hours making the counter tops, and worked extremely hard; he would not hire help since he believed that he and he alone could do a job good.

This would later prove to be a driving factor in every aspect of our world. I will never forget my dad coming home from work (usually at 10:30 or later) and walking in the door; my stomach would start to tighten, fear would grip my whole body, and I would hear my dad's straw hat hit the lamp table just inside the living room.

The scariest words to hear in our home were, "So how did it go today?" He would ask my stepmom, who was more than glad to start talking to deflect the attention away from her. My stepmom would usually start with, "Well, the boys ..." and continue with whatever had happened that day. The story would usually be that she couldn't get them to do the chores: milk goats, chop wood, bring in wood, change out sprinklers, dig ditches, fix fences, pull weeds, or take nails out of boards. There was always plenty to do whether summer or winter.

There was always work, always a project to complete, which was seldom done to our dad and stepmother's liking; and if it was done right, never did we hear a word of appreciation.

No matter what the crime was, how big or how small, she would continue until my father became enraged; then, he would ask, what about the two girls. I would start to tremble and shake with fear, especially if I knew there was something that she could say, such as we were found having the cattle take a nap, we didn't do the dishes fast enough, or didn't do any of the many chores expected. We were taken off one chore or job to be put on another. By the time she was through, my father would become even more enraged and would begin what he called the "discipline."

During the times my brothers slept in the house, all three slept in two sets of bunk beds. Their cries of, "I'm sorry" and, "I won't do it anymore!" screamed out in response to the beatings and my father's shouts, telling them they were "stupid" and "lazy piles of shit." Their pleas, their cries, and their screams will be in my mind forever. I would lie in my bed frozen, crying, and wanting to vomit.

My father would threaten to take their mattresses from them so they would have to sleep on the plywood. That is exactly what would happen; they would have their cotton mattresses taken away and be left with nothing but a piece of splintered plywood that was of course very hard and cold to sleep on. Sometimes with good behavior they would get their mattresses. "Good behavior" usually meant extra hard labor..

After my father was done beating, screaming, and belittling my brothers, it would be my turn. My father would pull me out of my bed, whipping me so hard that I would just go into survival mode. My pajamas never fit; it was hard to find anything to wear at night that was clean. I can still remember holding onto my pajamas so they wouldn't fall off while he beat me.

Ellie was seldom beaten and I praise God for that, as the few times my father beat her I thought I would lose my mind. I hated him so badly; I truly wanted to kill him. As much as I hated being beaten, screamed at, and called the names he called me, it was not as bad as seeing him hurt my sister. Even the pain of my older brothers was overwhelming, and they were not kind to me.

I longed for love, just to have someone be kind to me. I didn't really know exactly what that felt like, but I know that I was sometimes very sad in a way that I just couldn't explain. However, there wasn't much time to feel sorry for ourselves as our lives were very driven. I learned very early that I if I wanted to survive I had better pay attention and try to figure out how to make it through each day.

Chapter 5
School

I STARTED SCHOOL—FIRST GRADE—IN 1971; we didn't have kindergarten in that little town. I can remember my first grade teacher, Mrs. Brennan. She taught first through third, and her husband taught fourth through sixth grades. Mrs. Brennan was a good teacher, I suppose, but she smoked and drank coffee, and even at that young age, I found myself trying to avoid asking her questions so that I wouldn't have to have her stand over me and talk. The smell made me feel sick. I was very excited to learn, though, and did very well in spite of many situations present in my home life that made it almost impossible to engage my mind in school.

I have many memories of school, very few pleasant. School was a very emotional time. I wanted so bad to make a friend and in school that is sometimes very hard to do.

The Skull Valley School had only two classrooms, with a small library, a lunch room and two bathrooms: one for boys, one for girls. A hall separated the classrooms from the library and the lunchroom. In the hall, there was a bell and that is how school started and also ended: by the ringing of the bell. It was really a privilege to ring that bell; however, I only had that privilege maybe twice, as I was far too unpopular with both students and teachers.

The treatment from the school kids was so heartbreaking. It's very hard for me to put into words many of the Skull Valley happenings, both at home and school. Even today as an adult, I often feel overwhelmed by the life I was expected to forge each day. The workload alone was tremendous.

I would get up around six each morning, and that's where it all began, preparing to attend school. Early on, when I was very young, my stepmother tried to make sure my sister and I looked as good as possible for school. My stepmother tried to find the best at the Salvation Army and other thrift stores. I don't remember ever having anything new as a small child.

My younger sister had a very sensitive head and combing her hair was an issue every morning. I can still remember how angry I felt as I watched my sister crying and my stepmother combing her hair very roughly and telling her that, if she didn't stop crying, she would get Dad.

We often had chores even before school. In the fall, we'd pick up fruit that had fallen and bring it in to be canned. Then around January or February, the baby goats started being born and needed to be fed before school. Sometimes there were as many as twenty babies. The mothers had to be milked first, and then the babies fed. As we got a little older—nine and ten or so—my younger sister had to milk the goats before school also. Getting up at five thirty was necessary to get all the chores done by school time. Still we often missed the bus.

Nothing was very predictable in our home except fear, confusion, and chaos. So it makes it hard to bring a clear picture to paper for others to understand just what life was like in our home on a daily basis.

I only know that by the time I had completed my first year of school, I knew I had real problems on my hands. My stepmother had another baby and this baby was stillborn. I remember as if it were yesterday. I was so excited to see this baby. She was all dressed and wrapped in a blanket for us to see before she was taken away. She was very pretty with blonde curly hair. I was so sad when I learned she was dead, and I didn't really know what else to feel except extremely sad and lonely. I'm not sure exactly what happened to that little girl, but I was told it was a breach birth and that she died during delivery.

My father was almost always in a foul mood. I was overwhelmed by school, chores, fear of going to school, fear of coming home; fear surrounded me. I woke up to fear, lived fear, and slept fear. Fear was something I thought was a normal feeling: even though I hated it, it was there.

By the time I was in the second grade, it was clear that what I could expect was to get up very early, try to get whatever was expected of me done, and then try to find socks that matched, clean underwear, and something to wear. We were not allowed to wear pants except on very rare occasions, and it was hard to find a clean skirt and blouse or dress and tights in the winter.

None of the other kids dressed like me, and I was always made fun of. I felt sick every day as I boarded that bus, just waiting for the remarks that would be snarled out at me: "No you can't sit here; get away you stink," and yes, I did stink most of the time. I was allowed a bath once a week and I had a very bad bed-wetting problem. I wet almost every night. My bed-wetting would prove to be one of my living nightmares. After I was seated on the bus, I would try to ignore the other kids and just hope I could make it to the school as the bus traveled along the roads.

I would start to wonder how I was going to handle the recesses. Once the bus arrived at the school, I would have to deal with the free time before school started. Kids would hit me, throw rocks at me and call me "billy goat" or "pee pants Paula." I would feel so angry, sad, and overwhelmed that I would want to vomit.

I had brothers at the same school for a year or so, and then it was just Ellie and me there, but kids were so mean to me that even Ellie didn't want to be around me. For the most part, I just tried to hide. If I were forced by a teacher to play a game, I was the one no one wanted to have on their team, and a fight would break out because no one wanted Paula—she stunk.

On the rare occasions I had candy, I usually had stolen it from the teacher's drawer or the Skull Valley Store. I knew it was wrong, very wrong, but I knew other kids did it, and so to have the chance to have "friends" for even a few hours, I would do anything even if it wasn't right. That was a very large part of my life as a child.

The mornings dragged on at school and every recess was torture. I hated recess, and the older I got, the worse recess became.

Lunch was almost always a nightmare. My father had read that eating out of aluminum (the school cooked in aluminum) could make one wet the bed, and I wet the bed, so we had to take our own lunches. For whatever reason other than plain meanness, the school would not allow my sister and I to eat our sack lunch in the cafeteria with the other children. So, we stood at the doors of the cafeteria while the prayer was recited and then my sister and I had to eat in the library.

I hated being so alone, and yet I could hide out in my fear and pain. My sister and I hated our lunches, always packed in long, old bread bags that came from I don't know where, as we were given home-baked bread that often was really awful, sometimes rising to only about three inches high and very hard.

But that was not the worst. The bags smelled old with rancid peanut butter, and the thermos of milk had a glass insert that would break away from the edge of the thermos, letting old dish water get down the sides so that when you poured out the goats milk, the nasty water would come out into the milk.

I can remember the taste and smell to this day, and I can tell you that I went hungry many of those days. I would go to the bathroom, pour the milk down the drain and put the sandwich in the bottom of the trash can, making sure it was covered by paper towels, because if it was ever discovered that I threw away food, I would receive a severe beating.

At home, the food was better most of the time; at least the food we grew was very good unless my stepmother turned it into, well charcoal, and that was no excuse not to eat it. So many times food that started out good was ruined!

Then there was the issue of purchased foods such as oats and peanut butter. Even if the peanut butter was rancid, it was to be eaten anyway, with nothing said; the oatmeal, well, if it had become rancid and full of bugs, and you also had better eat it and say nothing! These foods were served almost daily, and many times I would just choose to go hungry, only taking and eating a very small amount.

I can still remember the times that our lunch would contain a few things I liked, such as canned fruit, or even raisin bread with margarine on it. I would hardly be able to keep my mind on the schoolwork. I would go to lunch and eat with such joy. Whenever my lunch was not rancid, soggy, or rotten tasting, it was a good day.

Recess after lunch was the longest recess, and often I would try to find a place to hide, as trying to play with the other kids always brought another chance for mean words or actions, and the pain as the years went by became unbearable. So I would hide out and wait. The bell was always a welcome sound and as I settled in my chair, I would hope that no one could smell me. I could smell myself all day and knew I needed a bath and clean clothes, but that just was not possible in our home.

Home: oh that sick spot would be back and fear would start to rise as I'd see the clock head toward 2:30 p.m.—the end of school—and what could be worse at the end of school than the bus ride back home. I would never know what was waiting there, and the fear, anxiety, and sickness in my stomach would grow as the bus got closer to home. What would I face, was Dad home? Was he mad? What had happened while I was gone? Since I hadn't been there to see and hear everything that happened I wouldn't know what to avoid or escape. I would walk in and face the unknown every day.

So, every morning I got on the bus and wondered what would happen, and who would be extra mean; every afternoon I returned home and would try to figure out what I needed to do to survive there.

One day when I was about nine, I felt I could no longer keep quiet when a girl, who was probably five years older than I was, called me "pee pants Paula." I turned around and yelled, "buck teeth Colleen!" I don't remember much of the following minute as I nearly blacked out when she hit me hard in the face. This happened on the school bus and the bus driver never even said a word to the girl.

Not only did the kids treat me with such disdain that I hardly felt human, but in the fifth grade I had a teacher, Mrs. Barbara, who also was the principal of the school and who I believe truly hated me. One day she had us raking the schoolyard. I can't remember all the details of what happened, but I know that an older boy started picking on me, and I just kind of lost it and started yelling. Mrs. Barbara grabbed me, took me into the school, and paddled me hard. I was so heartbroken that she had done that. I got home that night and told my mom, who told my dad, and to my great shock, he told me that if that teacher ever tried to spank me like that again, I should run home and he would take care of the teacher. I was in shock: for the first time in my life, my dad had stuck up for me! Wow!

So a couple of weeks later, when Mrs. Barbara told me that I was going to get a paddling—even though I truly don't remember why—I bolted from the room and ran outside to find my sister. My legs were shaking and my heart was pounding so hard I could hardly breathe. Panic set in as I realized I didn't know where she was on the playground, and Mrs. Barbara, with her beady eye glasses and quite large girth, was looking for me. I ran around our community auditorium, and there at the side of the building was my sister. I called to her, and just as I was telling her that I was running home because Mrs. Barbara was going to spank me, I noticed a look in my sister's eyes, but it was too late. As I turned to look, Mrs. Barbara grabbed me. The anger, fear, and frustration I felt were overpowering and I fought to get away. After all, for the first time in my life, my father had stuck up for me and said I didn't have to be mistreated by her again. As I fought, the teacher grabbed me, threw me on the ground, and proceeded to sit on me until I could no longer fight. All the other children were watching. I'm not sure what they thought but the humiliation I felt was so great I really didn't care.

After I quit fighting, she pulled me to my feet and toward the schoolhouse, where Mrs. Palmer was. Mrs. Palmer was an even larger woman but usually very kind. However, Mrs. Barbara was the principal, and she ordered Mrs. Palmer to help her hold me as I was given several swats with a large plywood paddle. Years later, I was given that paddle to keep.

After the spanking, I went home and told my father, and as promised, he went to the school and told the teacher she had better never touch me again. It's funny that somehow he felt justified to beat me but would not allow a teacher to do so.

Mrs. Barbara did not renew her contract with the school the following year and that suited me just fine.

It was heartbreaking to feel so rejected by the school kids, but it was devastating to realize that even my younger sister, whom I felt was the only person in the world who loved me, started finding it hard to be nice to me. She ignored me at school, for the most part, because I was such an embarrassment to her. It was even more than she could cope with to be around a person that others disdained so much. She just didn't know what to do.

I certainly knew what loneliness was; however, it was not my main focus: survival was, and I focused on it day in and day out. How I made it through school is amazing.

In the fourth grade, a new girl came to our school. She was very dirty and her hair—well, it stood out like a scarecrows hair sort of, but she was nice to me, and I was so thankful to have a friend that I didn't care if she scratched her head every few minutes. To me, she was wonderful; she was my new friend. Then she moved, but not before she shared her lice with me, and I shared them with a younger sister, my stepmother's third child.

As I was showering my little sister one night, I found a bug in her thin, blonde baby hair, and so I went to my stepmother. I really didn't know what it was, but I would soon find out. I had never seen lice before and oh, I truly wished, after they were discovered, that I had not now. I was the only other one who had them, and that was because I was such a bad child that these little demons had attached themselves to me: I was just a "demon in flesh."

I spent the next month having kerosene put on my head and left there until it burned my scalp so badly that sores appeared. Then my stepmother spent hours debugging me while my father yelled and called me names. My heart pounded, and I wished I could just run away. I was expected to do extra because I stayed home from school and had caused so many problems for the family. I was such a stinking pile of crap, a demon, and a good-for-nothing.

By the time I was nine, I had learned to make bread. Eight loaves of bread were baked every other day in our family. In the beginning, it was hard to make the two batches of bread: get up early and put whole-wheat berries in the electric grinder, and make sure you start the grinder first! Then start pouring the wheat in slowly—not too fast, or it will plug it and then—well, in a normal family, grace would be given, but not in ours. You had better fix it and fix it now, or there would be grounds for another beating. As a child, I figured out how to do many things out of fear.

After the wheat was done, two batches of bread were mixed up using half wheat flour and half unbleached, white flour. I learned how to make this bread during the month I stayed home because of the lice. It was a very scary time of guilt and fear. I felt it was my fault. If I just hadn't played with that other girl, I wouldn't have gotten lice and caused so much pain for my family. It was always my fault, and I really did want to be a good child. I prayed almost every night for Jesus to help me not be a demon so that my family would love me but it never seemed to work. I was just a "demon in the flesh," said my dad on a regular basis.

Every time we thought the lice were gone, they weren't, and the kerosene was applied and the treatment started over. I had the kerosene put in my head only about four times but the burning was so painful. With each infestation, the attention would shift back to me, along with all the same yelling, reminding me that if I weren't such a bad child, full of Satan, this wouldn't be. After all, no one but my younger sister, with whom I had to share a bed, and me got lice, and my sister's left right away. Only mine kept returning. This was proof that I was a demon.

Then the knock came on the door, and it was CPS, (Child Protective Services) asking why I wasn't in school. They were very kind and recommended a treatment that eliminated the lice after one application. I was very thankful to those wonderful people; however, I was yelled at and hit in the back of the head for causing the government to come to our home. The government, doctors, and anyone else that my father did not approve of, were very bad and we must never trust them.

By the time I was nine, hardly a day went by that I wasn't slapped, kicked, or called a stink or demon in flesh. Spankings came along with the above, and I never healed from one to the next. I would try to turn my bottom so that some of the pain was better distributed. Sitting in school was very hard to do some days, as the pain was constant.

Going back to school after being gone for a month with lice gave great ammunition to the other children. My hair had been cut off very short. School was extra painful for a very long time after that.

The other kids made even a bigger point not to sit with me, and when there was no room on the bus, the bus driver would force them to allow me to sit with them. I felt so filthy, dumb, and ugly from all the things that were sneered at me daily.

One day as I was hiding around the back of the school thinking I was safe, feeling lonely and very blue, a girl walked around the building. Her eyes landed on me but her expression never changed as she said, "Oh, it's only you, Billy." Again, I never smelled very good due to my lack of bathing and the bed-wetting problem I had. I was called "Billy" referring to a Billy Goat or male goat, as there are very few animals that smell worse, remember we had goats and the kids were not sure if I smelled from the goats or bed wetting.

Somehow, I made it through the fifth grade at the Skull Valley School—such a fitting name; it would be my last year there as the sixth grade would bring a very big change for me.

Chapter 6
Fear, My Constant Companion

FEAR IS NOT A FUN COMPANION but I just couldn't get it to leave me. I felt it day in and day out. I trusted no one and felt as if I was going to explode some times because there were so many areas in my life in which I could get into trouble at any time, and I never knew what was going to happen next.

I'm not sure when the bed-wetting started; I think I was around three. I was told that I potty trained well, but I was so young that I really can't remember.

The bed-wetting was one more situation I dealt with on a daily basis. Not only did the school kids make sure I knew I stunk, but my own family, especially my brothers, made me their focus of cruelty. They called me pee pants Paula and taunted me about how I must enjoy peeing the bed; how I'd lay there just waiting for the warm pee, enjoying all of it; and how I was just so lazy. They constantly made fun of me, belittled me, and told me how ugly I was; not normal brotherly fun, but mean, evil, hurtful teasing until I felt as if I would die.

My parents had other plans and ideas about my bed-wetting. I was lazy, they said. They tried every form of healing they could think of, from no water at bedtime to well … I'll share a few others:

Spanking me was a given; humiliation was always an answer. To highlight this: when I was about eight, I had to march into the living room every morning and announce whether or not I had wet the bed; well, forget the "or not"—it always happened. I can remember only a dozen times or so before I was twelve that I didn't wet the bed, and I didn't quit completely until I was married at sixteen.

I was then given the "choice" to either have a whipping or go see a doctor to find out what was wrong with me. Well, let me tell you, I wasn't going to see a doctor. I had heard how bad they were, how they just kill people, and that if you go to a doctor you did not believe in God. Well, I knew I did not want to die, and I sure *did* want to believe in God.

I was horrified as this treatment ran its course every morning for two or three weeks. At 2:00 or 3:00 a.m., I would realize I was wet again and pull myself out of bed, try to find something to put over the wet spot, try to find dry clothes, and then crawl back into bed and hope to sleep again.

Then morning would come, and I would wish I were dead: I would now have to confess. Would I try to hide my wet clothes and lie? Not during this "treatment," because I was sure that my stepmom would check as she always did and it would be even worse.

So, trembling, I would come out of the bedroom and walk into the living room. My father, sitting in his tan recliner, would look at me and his whole countenance would change to one of disgust. He would say, "Well?" and I would then have to say, "I wet the bed last night." I often thought I would pass out with fear. Then with his voice very flat he would ask, "Well, what is it going to be, a spanking, or the doctor?" Of course, I chose the spanking. Then he would get up out of his chair, get the black PVC pipe and as always, I would lie down and take eight to ten swats. The pain was so bad I could hardly get my breath, but I never fought my father. I was always compliant; never did I yell or run. I just took it.

I was never sure what would end each "treatment." I guess he just would get tired of whipping me. Every whipping came with words of belittlement: "lazy," "stupid," "what's the matter with you?" "Get your life right with Jesus and you won't have these problems." So I would pray and ask Jesus to help me, but nothing ever changed and the abuse continued.

Another treatment was that all the other kids in the family could have flannel sheets except Paula; I wet the bed, so being warm was not something I deserved. I never did get flannel sheets and I was always cold at night. We only had wood heat and that old house had no insulation; by morning, when the fire went out, I was so cold I hurt. I would be huddled so tightly into a ball that my muscles hurt and, of course, there was always a wet bed to try to sleep in.

Another treatment, when I was nine or ten, was to have me start a fire outside, put a big washtub on it, boil water, and hand wash all my clothes and bedding. I remember a loneliness that would engulf me as I filled the tub with water and waited for the water to boil. The fire and smoke would whip up around the edges of that pot as I waited, testing the water to see if it was hot enough to dissolve the powdered soap. After about an hour of putting wood on the fire, testing, and feeling as if I were the filthiest child on the earth, I would put my clothes in that water, find a cottonwood stick, and start stirring.

I had no idea how to wash clothes or how to make sure they actually got clean. I just poked and stirred. The pot was outside the kitchen window, so I knew I was being watched. I always felt watched: watched with a critical eye, one of complete disdain. Not once in my childhood years did I ever hear the words *good job* or *I love you*. Or even feel a kind touch that was really a kind touch.

After "washing" the clothes, I would pull them out with the stick and put them in a basket. I couldn't wring them out until they had cooled. Then I would empty the water, refill, and start the rinse. It took me several hours just to clean a few clothes, and they still smelled and were terribly stiff after drying. I'm sure the soap was still in them; stains also appeared on them if I didn't hang them up right away. I don't remember how long this treatment went on before it was decided that I could use the wringer washer and do, not only my clothes, but load after load after load of everyone's clothes and diapers. By the time I was nine, I had four stepsiblings and there was plenty of work to care for them.

The bed-wetting continued no matter what was done or what form of humiliation was used; however, my dad, stepmother and an older sister, who I felt never cared for me, came up with yet another plan. Even now, as I write this, I feel pain and sadness that anyone would carry out this next treatment.

Pants were very rare, wonderful apparel that, my sister and I were told, were sinful and were only worn on rare occasions, but in the fourth grade, for the purpose of a "treatment," I would have to wear to school a pair of blue, elastic-waist pants, with a diaper. It was not just any diaper, discretely worn under a full dress, but an orange and white striped one. I begged; *please* don't make me wear it–*please, please, please!*

My older sister and stepmother worked together to hold me down and pin a large bath towel on me, threatening to get Dad. The towel was striped orange and white—large stripes. The towel was so large it stuck up above the pants about two inches and filled the pants to the max. The shirt covered it only as long as I didn't move the wrong way, and that was impossible.

I don't know how I made it through that day, but the horror I felt was beyond words. I know the teachers knew that I was wearing a diaper as the kids made fun of me for it, and yet neither of the two teachers said a word to find out what was going on.

Most of the time, I loved the idea of wearing pants to school and it made me feel as if I were somehow a part of the other children. Everyone knew our family was somewhat strange: I smelled; we were not allowed phone calls because my dad said it made his heart jump for the phone to ring. Since it usually meant it had something to do with his business; we couldn't eat the same food as the other children or even eat in the same room; and we had no TV, so when other children spoke of TV shows, we had no idea about them. They knew that my sister and I herded cattle and that there seemed to be no end to the children being born into our family. The children were all born at home, never with a doctor or at the hospital, and the rumor became that the babies were born on the kitchen table; untrue, but painful, nonetheless. And you can't fight a half truth or rumor. The babies *were* born at home; with no doctor, and they just kept coming year after year.

Eventually there would be fourteen siblings younger than I, and six older that were my dad's biologically from three marriages. Then there were three older that were my mother's from her first marriage: a total of twenty-one for my dad, and twenty-four children, total.

But to have just one day in which I felt I belonged even a little, tiny bit felt so good, and for whatever reason, when I wore pants, I fit in a little bit.

The bed-wetting consumed me at night as a child. During the day, I had plenty of other fears and work to face, but when night came, I always had to face that bed. The bed was awful; it was a cotton mattress on a piece of plywood.

That bed had been wet so many times, and when the stench became unbearable, I would be ordered to drag the mattress through the house in front of the rest of the family, with my brothers saying how gross I was, that I was "pee pants Paula," and putting on a big show in their distaste for me. I would work very hard to get the foul smelling mattress out the door and thirty feet or so over to the double propane tanks that were by the shop, hoist it up there, and leave it to dry for several days. I would sleep on the plywood while my mattress "aired" and dried out.

After several years of constant wetting on this mattress, a large hole had actually rotted all the way through it. I would try to sleep at the other end, away from the hole. Even the plywood was black and rotted. It smelled no matter what; a good night for me was when the mattress was aired and dry. Although dry and aired certainly only reduced the odor but of course never got rid of it. I would bring it back in, put it on that rotten, stained plywood, and put clean sheets on it. I couldn't wait to get in that bed and pray. I prayed so hard I cried, asking Jesus not to let me wet the bed so I could wake up dry and not have to wake up around 2:00 or 3:00 a.m. to change my clothes, find a towel or dirty clothes to put over the wet spot, and try to go back to sleep. I was so tired at night that it was often hard to change and try to find a dry place to go back to sleep.

I remember often lying in bed at night, feeling like the only child in the world who wet the bed and wondering what really was wrong with me: it must be that I was a bad person. Even at that young age, I had started thinking about what could really be causing it.

I would tell God that, when I grew up and had children, I would never be mean to a child that wet the bed. I would play out in my mind how I would love such a child, change the bedclothes, bath them, and make sure that no one ever knew. I would hug the child and reassure them that I loved them. I longed so much to be loved, and ached to hear a kind word. I wanted to have just a single, solitary, itty-bitty nice word or kind touch. I was not vindictive as a child; I just wanted to be loved.

The beatings continued and became worse as time went on. It seemed that my father, who had "retired" at the age of forty (I was eight then), had become very available to bring down fear and beatings on a regular basis. It seemed nothing was ever right, and with so many children, he was always angry about something.

With no indoor toilet, potty chairs needed to be emptied, sometimes several times a day, as there were several children using them. One day, as I was trying to take one of the over-flowing pots out with my dad yelling at me, I spilled some on the floor. He proceeded to hit me so hard that the pee went all over. I'm not sure at what point it happened, but one of the blows made my lip bleed. As the blood started dripping on the floor, he ordered my stepmother to take the pot of urine from me, then hit me and yelled, "Quit getting blood on the floor!" I was numb with fear and just tried to get away.

My stepmother didn't say anything kind or try to protect me, but she did try to help me clean up the urine and blood. I would never have a clue when this type of anger would erupt, but I could rely on one thing: it was most every day. However; if the anger was not directed at me then it was another sibling that was targeted.

Clothes that I liked were certainly scarce, and all of my clothes either came from Goodwill or from boxes of old clothes that my stepmother kept in the attic. I have no idea if she got them from the thrift store or just kept them for us as we grew. I don't believe any of them were from my older sisters, as they were all much older. The closest in age was nine years my senior.

One of my stepmother's comforts was to buy clothes from the thrift store, but never would she return any, so as time went on, there were many boxes of clothes—and I mean many. They filled both attics upstairs, each probably ten by twenty feet, and a large area that was within the living room area upstairs. My stepmother would spend hours going through the boxes, rearranging and refolding all the clothes and pulling out a few for us kids to wear. One blouse that my stepmother found for me I really liked.

It was, for all fashion purposes, out of style for the time; however, I enjoyed it. It was a brown and tan check and fit my waist with a little flair at the bottom that really made me feel like a girl. I wore it often.

For many years, I had forgotten about this blouse and about what had happened to it, until my dear sister and I were talking and she said to me, "Paula do you remember the time outside, under the tree with the nightlight on it, when dad beat you so badly and ripped your shirt completely off of you?" I felt a rush of pain and fear as I realized that I had not thought about it since I was almost eleven. I had felt so exposed, and the one blouse I had liked so much was gone. I don't even know what I did wrong. I've tried many times to remember but I just can't. I hadn't felt that I had ever blocked anything that had happened to me before. Part of me wished it had stayed blocked.

My dad's anger had grown to a point that I often feared even for my life and the lives of my brothers, at times. His face would become red and he would scream and hit us while we begged, "Please, we won't do it again," hoping to appease him.

The offense could be as small as bringing home clay from school, as my sister once did. That was the only time I remember her being badly beaten. I'm not sure how old she was, but I believe around nine. She brought clay home from school, even though she had been told not to. I'm not sure why she did, except there were few toys in our home and just to have a little something to play with was a great temptation.

I still remember when my stepmother told my dad that my sister had brought home the clay anyway; as my dad entered the bedroom, my sister backed up into the closet and then the beating began. He started hitting her, knocked her down and, as she lay on the floor, he kicked her in the crotch time and time again. Her screams made me feel I would go crazy. I really wanted to hurt him and if not for the fear, I probably would have done something that would have gotten me beaten also.

The beatings and bed-wetting seemed to go hand in hand, and the more beatings I received, the more I wet; a vicious cycle that wouldn't end.

Chapter 7
The Dark Secret

I LOVE PEOPLE and have always wanted people to love me. I believe that has just been my nature from birth. It is a great nature in a safe, loving family that cares for one another and protects one another.

Well, not in my family. There was the life that people saw from the outside—a large family with some strong religious views and a dad who was strict. But was there really anything strange? Only we knew the depths!

Our family had levels of sickness and levels of abuse that we all witnessed and experienced daily. There was also a deep, dark secret that started small and then grew and grew until it consumed our whole family.

I don't even remember the first occurence, but by the time I was four, I realized there were things that my older brothers had me do to them, and that they did to me, that made me feel very sick. It just seemed strange, and I didn't like it. Plus, I really didn't like their double standard: nice to me when they got me alone, but when we were around everyone else, why were they so mean? I just didn't understand, and I had no problem keeping it to myself, as it seemed rather icky and gross. But for a brief moment, kindness was shown to me and I needed it so badly. I didn't realize at that age how I was being programmed and used by my brothers.

I'm not sure when my dad discovered that my brothers were abusing me sexually, but I remember my dad giving them a sound beating and telling me to stay completely away from them. And so the cycle began.

The first couple of times, just my brothers received the beatings for the sexual abuse, but by the time I was six, I was considered part of the problem, and every few months when my stepmother would catch my brothers, we would all receive a beating. I felt very confused. It was the only way to have my brothers show kindness. I was promised things such as candy or gum, and they would smile at me and not be mean for a few minutes.

At first, after being caught and beaten, my brothers were cold, mean, and downright nasty to me in every way. It was as if they truly were trying to not repeat the same sin by treating me—who, in their minds, had caused the problem in the first place—with utmost disdain. They called me pee pants Paula, ugly, and stupid, and told me that I stunk: whatever it took to belittle me and I guess make themselves feel more powerful.

Then the decline to abuse would start with a remark such as, "If I give you a piece of gum, would you help me take the wood into the house?"—or feed the baby goats, or milk the goats, or pull these weeds ... Of course I would agree, not only for the promise of gum, which I knew I would more than likely never see, but because I longed so much for a word of kindness, just one. I truly believed that if I helped them and was kind, maybe they wouldn't make fun of me anymore and would find value in me.

For whatever sad reason, I believed that when my brothers got into trouble for sexually abusing me, it would be the last time they would ever even try such a thing again. So, with that belief in mind, I would accept the kind word or gesture and work, only to find out that the next step was already being planned. The trap was set, and

I, being so hungry for love and approval, couldn't say no. I just went along, knowing all too well that I was back in the trap.

My brothers could treat me however they wanted; they could be kind or cruel to me and make me allow the sexual abuse. I didn't dare say no. The trap went like this: after I was involved, I had to play the game because if my dad found out, we all would be beaten. The other part of the trap concerned my oldest brother who lived at home at the time; he was a very cunning person who cared only for what he wanted.

He was the one who abused me the most and was the cruelest to me by far of all my brothers. When he wanted me to do something sexual, he would say, if you don't do this I'll tell dad that you did this, or that, or talked about our family's secret food supply. Whatever it took, he knew how to work it so that I would feel *trapped* like a helpless animal and would just do it.

One time that really stands out in my mind is the time I finally decided to stick up for myself. I had had enough and I knew that I was not going to let my brother hurt me again. I was nine or ten and there was no way I was going to take the fall again. I told my older brother, when he tried to con me into sex, that I was not going to do it no matter what, and he said, "Oh really. Well, let's just see." He told me he was going to tell my dad that I had told the neighbors that my dad ate steak and ice cream in front of us and that we were not allowed to have any.

Well that story was partly true, as my dad *did* eat ice cream in front of us and we were not allowed any. However, I would have never done such a thing. I knew that and felt very comfortable in the fact that I was safe.

So, mustering up all the guts I had, I said, "go ahead, tell Dad because I didn't do it and I'm not doing anything else for you." I will never forget how I truly felt that I had made a new start and could finally tell him no, and that he would figure out that I could stand on my own two feet! A few hours later, that feeling was just a memory as my dad came at me with all the anger of a mad man and asked me, "So you think you can tell the neighbors that I eat steak and ice cream in front of you!" I froze completely, but I did muster up the strength to say, "No I didn't say that." Then my dad asked my older brother, "Did the neighbors tell you that's what she said?" and of course, he said yes. I was mortified as my dad came at me screaming that I was a liar and repeating his favorite name for me that was by now something I had heard far more than my name: you "demon in the flesh." I don't know what hurt more, the words or the beating; however the words that came with all the beatings took me years to heal from.

My brothers, especially the oldest at home at the time, had me and there was no way out. There were times I felt so trapped, but a small ray of hope was that my younger sister could tell them no and they didn't push it with her. My dad found more favor in her, and her beatings were few and far between. I was so thankful for that because to see her hurt was too much for me.

Another power my brothers carried was the power of Scripture; yes, Bible Scripture. Remember, we were a religious family. God was preached day in and day out. How we had better get right with Jesus or we would be headed straight for hell and would go through the great tribulation, be beaten and killed, tortured to death, starved and all manner of horrible things. With all that in my mind and trapped by my brothers, I wanted to be right before God, and so when my brothers said that the Bible said it was okay for them to do these things to me, I didn't know how to say no. It somehow, for the moment, gave me a sense of peace. I needed a little moment of peace sometimes so badly that I felt I sold my soul to them. I thought this would never end in my life; it seemed to go on forever.

I thought I would be forever caring for the cattle, fearing school and the kids, fearing coming home and working until exhausted, and washing buckets and buckets of dirty diapers for younger siblings outside in the cold with the water hose. My hands and arms would hurt so badly from the cold that I would want to vomit. I felt I was forever being trapped by my brothers, beaten, and called "demon in flesh."

Then there was the new rule that took the last bit of hope, the last bit of anything I may have had to fight that family. The new rule stated that any family member could hit, kick, slap, or call me whatever they wanted anytime they walked by me. And some of them took the liberty and enjoyed it. One might ask why. To this day I really don't know, but as I lay in bed at night, still wetting and carrying that burden, I would cry out to God and beg Him to help me, please help me be the person that I need to be. Help me not to wet or upset these people any more. I know I am a bad person, I must be; I don't know why, I just am. Please, please, please help me. I just want to be loved; please let someone say a kind word.

Not once during my first eleven years of life did anyone ever say, "I love you" without adding, "that's why I whip you"—my dad's only way of saying I love you. Never kind words such as, "You are a pretty girl," or, "You did a good job," or, "Thank you," or, "I love you." Just I love you; oh, to hear I love you! Just to have arms of love put around me. Even as I write this, I am painfully aware of how I felt then and the tears won't stop. What could make anyone feel they have the right to hurt another human being, even a stranger, in the way I was? But I was no stranger; I was their daughter and sister.

But, just as I thought there was no hope, my life changed in a big way.

Chapter 8
Oklahoma

NOTHING BROUGHT MORE EXCITEMENT TO OUR HOME than company. Company was very rare. Once a year was pretty much the frequency of company to our home, and even though that meant days and days of hard work to bring about some sort of cleanliness and order, they were worth it. We would work very hard, usually with several kicks, slaps, or even a major beating, but it was all worth it to see someone besides the family we lived with.

We rarely left home other than to go to school and on an occasional trip to town. That was about the extent of outside influence. There was no phone that we children were allowed to use and TV, well, that was just a tool of Satan not allowed at all. So, company meant two things: other people to look at and maybe hear a kind word from, and also a reprieve from my father's anger. For a short time, we were safe, unless we did something he didn't like, and that could be anything from not listening to what he was saying if he was talking, to not doing our chores fast enough.

While the company was there, he would point his finger at you and you knew that when they left you were doomed. So the rest of the time you were sick to your stomach and even though you wanted the company to stay, you felt too sick to enjoy them; but you also didn't want them to leave because you knew what was coming.

But this time my sister Sue, her husband, and her baby were coming! Oh, I could hardly wait! This sister loved my younger sister and me. She was my mother's second-to-oldest daughter and had moved to Oklahoma to live with an aunt after my mother died. She was my ray of hope. She sent dolls every year for our birthdays and Christmas, even though I never played with those dolls and neither did my sister, as we felt funny playing with dolls. What did you do with dolls? We had no idea how little girls did that.

We played with cattle, bugs, birds, rocks, sticks, and little toy animals, but mostly we worked. We only played when on the road with the cattle. Once I did play with a small doll for a short time, and tried to sew clothes for her. That was kind of fun, but only for a very short time. But to look at the dolls gave my sister and me great joy, and both of us had decided that we would give them to our daughters when we grew up. So deep in our hearts we had a future joy.

When Sue arrived, I was so excited to see her. She was tall, very tall, and very beautiful, and her daughter was so cute: just a beautiful little girl and so small. Sue was different: she seemed worried about something.

Someone suggested we go swimming in our reservoir that was kept quite clean for swimming. The outside of our home was always better cared for than the inside. As we started up toward the reservoir, Sue said she was worried about her hair falling off. I just couldn't understand why until she dove in the reservoir and off came her hair. I realized it was a wig, and under that wig was a small amount of hair left after her cancer treatment for non-Hodgkin lymphoma.

I had no idea what that disease was or what she was going through. She was still very kind and said all the things I so badly needed to hear. "I love you, do you know that, Paula?" she would say, and because my name was rarely used in any positive way, or used at all, it was hard to hear my name. It felt rather strange, I knew I didn't like my name; it was attached to a girl I didn't like much, me. Sue told me how pretty I was and that really made me feel uncomfortable also, but I still needed to hear it and I liked her a lot.

It was only days until my eleventh birthday, and I was very excited to think that Sue would be there for that. Maybe it would be special, and maybe I would get a cake and ice cream. I hoped but I tried not to hope too much. It only hurt to hope.

I heard my father and my sister talking one day and I realized they were talking about me: Why me? I had to listen to find out. It was very painful to hear my father tell my sister what a horrible child I was. I wet the bed, I lied, I was more than he could handle, and he felt I was a demon or demon-possessed. I was so overwhelmed by what I heard.

I'm not sure if my sister asked to take me or if my father asked her to take me, but it was soon decided that I was going to live with my sister, her husband and baby in Oklahoma. Oh, was I excited, scared and beside myself. This was August 1976, and my life was going to get so much better, I was sure. But how would I act and what would I do with my bed-wetting? I had no idea. I was free of my dad and brothers, so life had to get better.

We were to leave the day of my eleventh birthday, and even though I was excited, I wished my sister Ellie could come with me. I already knew I would miss her, and my heart ached for her.

My younger sister Ellie told me later that in some ways when I left, she felt sad but in others, she was glad. It wasn't that she really believed that I was a "demon in the flesh," as I was called, but part of her knew something was wrong and maybe my father was right! All she knew was that she felt a relief because the problem was gone, so their life would be better. Ellie told me this shortly after I started this book. I realized even as an adult, not just through the eyes of a child that I had truly been abused and rejected by my whole family. My father had warped even the mind of my younger sister. I was singled out, and I will never know why.

The day we left, which was my birthday, my stepmother went to my father and I heard her ask, "I know its Paula's birthday and she's leaving today, but can she wash out the diapers before she leaves?" My father's words were, "get as much out of that no-good-for-nothing demon in the flesh as you can before she leaves." So I washed out three very large buckets of diapers that day; so much for the hopes of a wonderful birthday!

A few clothes were packed for me and we left. What I didn't know was that, going back with us in the red Chevelle were my oldest sister on my mother's side, Louise; her little boy; Sue; her husband and their little girl, and I. It was crowded but I didn't care. I was going to a new place!

The first day was okay; we drove and drove. I had never been in a car that long and as we drove, I realized I needed to use the bathroom, but I was too afraid to tell anyone. I was in so much pain and so bashful, I didn't know what to do. It was so hot in that car that I'm sure some of it sweated out of me as time went on. I was exhausted—so many new things, even a stop at a Sonic for dinner. I had never eaten outside of my home except school sack lunches, or maybe a snack while in town once or twice a year. To eat a hamburger, French fries and a soda pop—oh my goodness, this was too much!

I was so tired after eating I couldn't stay awake, and I thought the urge to use the bathroom had been put away, but once I fell asleep, I wet. I realized, when we stopped at the motel to sleep, that I had wet, and I was mortified. I wanted to die. I could run but I couldn't hide. I don't remember how it was handled, but I'm sure my sister was kind. She only became frustrated over it later. The hotel room was so noisy, but the little foldup bed I was on was okay. The air conditioner was awful. I had never heard such a thing and I froze all night. I didn't sleep a wink. What if I wet? What would I do?

After we arrived at my sister's house in Oklahoma, I was relieved but it soon became apparent that not all was bliss in this home either, and my two sisters fought so much that the older sister left. I'm not sure how she got back to Arizona, but I know that the dog, Lady, and I became fast friends. When we arrived at the house, there was such violence that Lady's dog house became a welcome place to go until it all cleared out.

I will be forever grateful for many good things at my sister's home. The home was clean; I had my own room with a double bed that was clean, not rotted with pee. Yes, there was plastic on it but that was fine; I felt much pressure not to wet and I woke up many mornings, at first, dry. It was a wonderful feeling!

There were foods I had never eaten before. Tacos, lasagna, fried okra, iced tea, Dr. Pepper to drink, fresh cow's milk—not goat milk—and graham crackers and cookies. A trip to Tulsa meant Taco Bell! I was delighted! Clothes my sister bought me, new clothes! I loved them! New socks, shoes, and panties!

We went to church and I met other family members, such as Aunt May, my mother's sister. I also met Aunt Kathryn, who, I later learned, was dying from lymphoma, That meeting was sad because I didn't really understand her sickness, I just knew she was very small and frail looking, though very pretty. When she got very ill, my sister would sit by the hospital bed that had been put in her living room, holding her hand and crying. I really couldn't understand at all; I just knew it made me really sad. She died about 8½ months after I met her.

It was only about 1½ months after I arrived at my sister's house that she announced she was pregnant and going to have a baby. It was the first time I had ever been told that a baby was on the way. It was something that, in my home, we weren't supposed to notice, so we pretended we didn't know that my stepmother was pregnant. Therefore, when my sister explained she was going to have a baby, I felt a little odd and didn't know how to react.

I didn't understand the fear in my sister's voice as she spoke to me about the pregnancy, either, until later when I heard her talking to my brother-in-law, her husband, telling him that the doctor had told her not to get pregnant for quite a long time. The cancer treatment she had undergone could cause her to abort the baby, or the baby could be mentally or physically handicapped. In addition, she could get cancer again.

So I would watch my sister, with that fear, try to care for her husband, daughter, and myself. I had problems in school and I was severely behind in all my subjects. I had done quite well in my school in Arizona; however, it was not as advanced as the school I attended in Oklahoma, so I had a very difficult first quarter. Both my sister and brother-in-law worked with me, trying to get my grade levels up.

When I look back, it was such a tough time on my sister. She really wanted the best for me; however, as she became more stressed about my grades, she confined me to the storage area to study, and it was very scary.

I was alone for hours in that storage area; the winter was very cold and that made it hard to study. My bed-wetting returned almost nightly and my sister's frustration grew. I felt the only answer was to do what I had done at home: try to hide my wet clothes until I could take them out and wash them when my sister was gone.

Well, that only led to anger on her part and fear on mine, of course, and a vicious cycle began. One night she informed me that every time I wet, my underwear would be saved, and then she would put it all together and tie it around my neck on a string for the night. I was horrified! I felt so helpless. Still, it was better being here than elsewhere. I had only received one spanking and no sexual abuse; life really felt pretty good!

I didn't hear from Ellie during the ten months I was gone except maybe once. There were no phone calls from my family that I know of, and I didn't call them, either. I had no desire to, except to talk to my younger sister.

One very cold morning in February, there was frost over everything. I had made my way to the bus stop that was about one hundred feet from the house when I realized that Lady, our Australian shepherd, had all kinds of dogs running after her. I knew she must be in heat. As I considered what to do, I could hear the bus about one-quarter mile away. I knew I had to alert my sister to the situation, so I started to run toward the house. The frost made it very slippery, but my only thought was that I just had to get to the house and then back for the bus.

As I reached the porch that was being built, I jumped up on the side, lost my balance and down I went. I landed hard! I felt a horrible pain in my arm but I thought, oh, you're all right. As I got up, I realized there was real pain. I went into the house and to my sister's bedroom. Startled, she sat up, her very pregnant belly making it hard for her to move. I was crying by now. I told her about the dog, and that I had fallen and my left arm hurt very badly. I don't think she knew what to think or do.

Not that she didn't know how to: she was a nurse. The problem was how to handle the whole situation as far as my dad and finances were concerned. She looked my arm over and couldn't see anything, but to move it caused more pain than I could bear.

So she did the dreaded deed and called my dad. As my sister talked to him, I became painfully aware, by the one-sided conversation, that what my dad was saying was very painful for her. She already hated this man with all the hate she could muster and never was shy about expressing it, although she was also scared to death of him.

I can remember my sister saying, "I don't know how you can say that about her, and, yes, she really needs to see a doctor, and I'll take her anyway." My stomach sank to the bottom. I hurt so badly physically, and I realized that I was still nothing to him.

My sister put the phone down and told me just to wait while she got ready. She put my niece in the car and then the most painful ride of my life started. The roads in Oklahoma are very bumpy and I felt every bump, every railroad track, and every stop and start.

We arrived at the little hospital about eight miles from where we lived and were told that I had a very serious collarbone break. We hadn't even thought to look that far up. It was coming through the skin and broken completely in half, so we were sent to a bigger hospital in Tulsa.

I had never been to a doctor in my life, and I was terrified. I knew doctors were bad people and that I had to be a bad person for being there. It only took me a short time, however, to realize that they wanted to help me, and their kindness was unmatched. It was good to hear the doctor explain that I wouldn't need surgery and that there was a new way of handling collarbone breaks; all that was needed was a brace. I thought, this is simple! Oh, what a surprise!

The brace was put on me and the doctor's knee went into my back. As he cinched the brace tighter, his knee pressed harder until my shoulders were pulled back very straight. The pain made me want to vomit but not one sound came out of my mouth other than a small groan. When the doctor was done, he looked at me and asked, "Are you all right?" Then he turned to my sister and said he had never seen even a grown man, even a football player, who did not scream.

He just didn't know that I had learned not to say a word when I hurt; it only led to more pain, such as the time when I was nine. I had been pushing my younger sister on the tricycle. I had been told to do it, and after pushing until I was hot and tired, I pushed the tricycle over to a lawn chair. As I sat down, I put my hand down first, grabbing the tubing that makes up the frame of the lawn chair. This particular lawn chair was made so that the bottom part folded back, and I put my right hand too close to the fold as I sat down, As my middle finger started to feel the pinch, I pulled my hand out and nearly tore off the top part of my finger.

In horror, I ran to the house. I was so scared: the top of my finger hung barely by a flap of skin, my nail was torn off and sticking up, and blood was everywhere. I ran into the house crying. My stepmother ran cold water over it in the kitchen sink; the pain was so unbearable I let out a few loud cries, and I was told to shut my mouth. I knew I had to, so I made as little noise as possible while an older sister and my stepmother pushed my finger back together, tried to put the nail in place, and wrapped it. I was so scared of my dad's reaction, as I well should have been. His first words were. "If you weren't such a demon, that wouldn't have happened to you; you deserve it. It's because you have been such a horrible child."

I couldn't wash dishes for a while, so other things were found for me to do: sort, hang, and fold laundry. My finger was so painful at night I couldn't sleep; no pain medication was ever allowed, not even aspirin. I had to soak my finger in disinfectant to keep the infection out. My fingernail eventually fell off and, after months, it grew back.

Or the time that I picked up a shovel and somehow shoved a large splinter under the nail bed of my thumb, it went the entire length of my thumb nail. I ran in the house looking for my stepmom and was told to shut my mouth as my dad was sleeping, so I was taken out behind the garage and my stepmom proceeded to pull it out with tweezers. Oh the pain, I fought passing out. I was instructed not to make a sound as that may wake my dad. Believe me I never made a sound!

Before I went to Oklahoma, I never wanted my dad to know when I got hurt because it was always deemed my fault: "It's because you're such a demon in the flesh."

I later found out that the day I broke my collarbone, my dad had told my sister to call him back to let him know if I had really broken my arm. She never did, because he had told her that day that if Satan hadn't ruled my life, and if I weren't such a demon in the flesh, it wouldn't have happened to me. I had sort of figured that had been said that day, because when my sister got off the phone, she had had anger in her eyes, and I had heard her say how much she hated that man. My dad had caused her great pain also, but I didn't know how at that time.

My collarbone healed ever so slowly, and there was a huge lump where the break had been; it wasn't until I was almost thirty that I could no longer feel where it had broken, and it was even longer before the pain went away entirely. But the pain of my dad's words took even longer to heal, longer than any of my physical pains.

The ten months I lived with my sister were the best months of my childhood. I learned that I could live clean, and I didn't have to smell when I was in school. Even though my sister didn't handle everything perfectly, I still felt more love from her and my brother-in-law than I had ever felt before.

My body changed a lot during those ten months, and I went from a little girl of about ninety pounds to a young woman of one hundred and twenty pounds. I grew several inches and filled out in every way. I felt very self-conscious in many ways, but I always felt safe with my sister and brother-in-law, especially sexually; it made it a wonderful time.

My older sister, however, must have worried about me being taken by my dad and would ask me sometimes if he had ever touched me. At first I said no, as I was too scared to tell the truth, but as time went on, I told the truth about what my brothers had done to me and about an episode when my dad touched me. I really didn't want to talk about it because so much fear came up in me when I did. I knew if he ever came back and found out, I would be in great danger, so I dreamed about how he would never come back and I would live happily ever after.

My sister wanted to see if she could keep me with her permanently. She had expressed this to me and was trying to figure out how to do it. Her very complex pregnancy and our very sick aunt made it very hard for my sister to reach into all the corners of her life.

But, as a child who had experienced little joy, fun, or freedom, I thought as little about my family in Arizona as possible, except for my younger sister Ellie.

I was excited about school ending that year; my grades had improved so much that my teachers complimented me often. I even received an award for most improved student!

I knew my aunt was very ill, but I hardly even thought about that; I knew my sister was going to have her baby any day, and I could hardly wait. My life felt so good. Then my aunt died, and my sister decided I shouldn't go to the funeral, but rather I should watch my niece, and that was fine with me. I was feeling so happy that I rarely wet the bed.

Summer was here, and it was beautiful. My sister's in-laws had horses that I was able to ride sometimes. I learned how to shoot a gun, fished in small ponds and ate wonderful meals with mostly happy people.

Then one morning in late May, after school had ended, I was told that my nephew would be born the next day. I had waited for him for so long; I was so excited my heart was dancing. A baby, one that I wouldn't have to take care of all the time and hand wash diapers for.

Life was so good until about 11:00 a.m. that day, and then all the horror I could possibly feel was there at once, as I looked out the window and saw my dad's yellow Volkswagen pull up. My heart raced, as did my mind. What was he doing here? Why didn't he let us know he was coming? Would I really have to leave? Surely, my sister could save me, and talk to him and ask that I stay with her. After all, I was doing so well there, and I wasn't too much of a problem. I grasped at straws in my head as I hoped against hope that this was a bad dream.

Then I froze inside and all emotions shut down. I don't remember if my sister let him ring the doorbell or if we went out. I just know that soon we were all talking. I realized the older sister, who had helped hold me down to put the diaper on me, was there, along with her baby that she had had while I was gone.

My dad, sister, and brother-in-law talked for a while. I don't really remember the conversation, as I had shut down. All I remember was,

"Yes, she has to go with me and she needs to pack now. We will leave as soon as she is packed."

I remember asking my sister to ask my dad if we could stay until the baby was born the next day; after all, I had been there the whole pregnancy. I was so excited about this baby. But the answer was no, we had to leave immediately. I shut down all feeling as best I could, packed what I could, as there was limited space, hugged my weeping sister and my very solemn brother-in-law, and we left. I felt my life was over, and in many ways, it was.

Chapter 9
Return of the Dark Secret with a New Twist

I'M NOT SURE HOW LONG WE DROVE IN SILENCE. My dad was driving, my sister and her baby were in the passenger seat, and I sat behind my sister. When my dad had arrived, there had been no affection, just a cold acknowledgment of me, and the sister who was with him just said, "Hi," in a very strange way.

Now I was riding with them in very cramped close quarters. My legs started to hurt within one hundred miles, but I knew better than to say a word and just tried to think the only happy thought I had: that I would see my younger sister, whom I had missed terribly.

I must have fallen asleep at some point, but I was awakened by my sister giving a strange little laugh and by my dad's voice. I remember opening my eyes and watching the two of them, at first feeling very confused at what I was seeing. Was I really seeing this right? What was going on? My mind raced again, and I felt a very icky, mixed feeling.

Then as I put it all together, I felt fear. There was no mistaking what I was witnessing: my dad was looking under the blanket my sister had over her, watching while she nursed her baby. I felt sick at the look in his eyes as he said little sexual things to her. I tried not to move too much, as I was afraid, very afraid. If he realized I knew what he was doing, would he hurt me again?

Then he reached over, touched my sister's breast and asked her sexual things. I was sick and so full of fear. He had beaten my brothers for abusing me sexually; what was he doing? Then the very ugly truth came to me. I had told my sister in Oklahoma about the time before I had left to live with her that he had made me sit on his lap while he sexually abused me, although he later said it was to check to see if I was still a virgin! What would I do?

I knew I didn't want to be hurt anymore, and here I was in a car headed back to the hell hole I had been rescued from. Would the beatings start again? What would I do about the bed-wetting? What would I do about my brothers? What would I do about my stepmother, who would do anything to divert attention from herself? I was a perfect target. I truly couldn't bear the thought, not for one minute. What will I do? I really didn't know, but I did know one thing: my dad seemed awfully nice to my sister. As we drove along, he flirted, played, and touched. I felt so sick but acted as if I had no clue as to what was going on.

We stopped a couple of times to use the bathroom, but other than that, it was a straight-through drive. I was given some food; however, I don't remember what. I was back in survival mode and would live there for many years to come.

When we arrived, I felt very strange. I had changed very much: I had left weighing eighty-nine pounds and returned weighing one hundred and twenty. I measured five feet four inches tall. My body had left a little girl and had returned a young woman.

My younger sister had not changed as I had, and when she saw me, I really can't say I saw happiness in her eyes. More of a nervousness, I suppose, that had to do with the fact that when I had left, she had felt relief, knowing that the person who had caused so much anger in the family was gone. Now I was back, and no one knew how I would affect the family again. All they remembered was that I was a "demon in the flesh," and while I was gone, there had been a little peace in the family, since I wasn't being regularly beaten and screamed at.

However, there was no need for anyone to fear that I was going to be beaten as I once had been, or yelled at and called a demon in the flesh. I would make sure of it. I knew I never wanted to be beaten or called names again, so I was going to be the best young girl I could possibly be. But what would that entail? I had learned that, when my dad was flirting and playing with my sister, he seemed very loving in a way that made me feel very sick to my stomach; still, he seemed nice.

Oh, how I longed to find favor in the eyes of that man, for him to say a kind word to me! I needed kindness and love so much that if I had to sell my soul, I would do it. I know I didn't see it that way then: that is, as selling my soul; however, when I looked back years later, I was very worried that I had done just that. But God showed me differently.

I became very aware of my body very quickly. The clothes that I had arrived in and had worn while at my sister's, were deemed very sinful, as they caused men to lust after me. I had pants on, and shirts that were considered too tight.

Well, my brothers noticed me right away. The one who noticed me the most this time was Sam. He gave me little icky smiles every time he saw me and made comments about my body.

I tried to ignore him and did for quite a long while, but my dad became a new problem just a few days after I arrived home. He called me out to the grape arbors, made me sit in his lap, and started asking me questions. I knew sitting in my dad's lap was not a good thing, and my heart nearly stopped. But he spoke with kindness, even though it gave me a sickening feeling. I knew what was coming, but I would never have told him no. I soon realized that if I let him do sexual things to me, he not only treated me "nice," but he also stopped calling me a demon in the flesh and beating me.

My dad sexually abused me for the following three years. I felt so much confusion during that time. I wanted to feel normal, but nothing was normal. I felt filthy, oh, so filthy!

Yet, as my dad would talk to me about sex and tell me how it wasn't wrong, I wanted so much to believe him. I knew in my heart it was wrong, but I couldn't tell him that. If I played the game, I was treated very well; in fact, I was put on a pedestal, in a way.

I still worried every day that I if didn't conform and be the "loving" girl that was expected, being helpful and working for hours to clean, cook, and care for the younger siblings, I would end up right back where I had been. I hated the sex, but I also hated being beaten, and I hated being a demon in the flesh.

I started seventh grade in the fall after coming back, but it was difficult. I was bussed twenty miles on a very large bus with many other kids from seventh to twelfth grades. It was a horrible time, as I had to see many of the kids who had tormented me during my first through fifth grade years. I tried to stay away from them and would end up being put in seats with the "freaks" (as they were called) of the bus.

It wasn't long after starting to ride the bus that a twelfth grader who I was forced to sit with started trying to touch me, and I was too scared to say no. He was showing me attention. He wasn't mean and he told me how cute I was, in fact. I was somewhat infatuated with him: he had long hair, was on drugs, and was very freaky, but he was nice to me. All it took was a kind word and I would let anyone do anything to me.

From the moment I left Oklahoma, I stepped back into living a double life. While living with my sister I had gained enough security within myself that I was learning I didn't *have* to live a double life. It felt good, and I didn't feel as much fear; however, I still felt as if something bad could happen at any moment. I lived with that feeling every moment with my dad and my family. I find it very difficult to pen my feelings or the happenings of the first three years after returning from Oklahoma.

The first year back, I know that I went to school and started living one life there and one life at home. At school, I tried to fit in with whoever would let me, and that was not such a great bunch of kids. Even my school life was split. In the classroom I tried to be the very good student—I was even in chorus and I loved it—but out of the classroom I tried to smoke, helped other kids steal from convenience store, and tried to prove I was really cool.

However, it is hard to do that when you are scared to death that your dad will find out and probably beat you. I really had to live a very compartmentalized life. I was one person in the classroom, another around my friends, and a totally different person at home. In fact, if a person from school would have dropped by my house one day, I'm sure that person would have been very shocked.

I was not allowed to wear pants to school unless I wore a dress over them, and believe me, it was not in fashion. When I was in the seventh and eighth grades, out of desperation, I would wear skirts over my pants, get on the bus in the morning, and take my skirt off and put it in my bag. Then on the ride home, I would put it back on just before getting to the bus stop in my hometown. That twenty-mile ride home had become just as sickening as when I was in grade school, only instead of being beaten, I was now afraid that, if I said no, I would fall from grace in my dad's eyes, and then he would start the beatings again. I worried constantly; fear was my constant companion.

My chores at home, of course, no longer included cattle grazing; however, there was plenty to take the place of cattle. My stepmother had now given birth to five children, and another was on the way. She did any and everything she could to keep from doing any more than she had to. She sat for hours nursing her baby, whichever one was the baby at the time. I can still see her: one leg pulled up slightly under the other one, one foot rocking the chair, the baby covered with a blanket, and a book in her hand. She would sometimes stay there for hours at a time. After having children of my own, I realized that she was just sitting and rocking the baby while I did the work.

I wasn't making bread during the school year at that time, as I had to be to the bus stop by 7:00 a.m. The bus stop was about a mile away and a bicycle was what got me there, unless it was raining too hard, and then sometimes I would get a ride.

I never really thought much of the bike ride except when it was still dark as I rode, or when it was extremely cold. Some mornings, the temperature would only be about nine degrees, and the wind would be blowing. As I said, I didn't mind so much; however, one day as I went under the railroad pass, I felt a very sharp pain in my back, as if I had been stabbed. I had been sick with a pain that wouldn't go away, and the cold made it hurt all day. But this morning it was worse than ever, and I lost consciousness, fell, and wrecked my bike. I really injured myself on the way down.

I was only out a very short time, and when I came to, I realized I had to go back home, bleeding and bruised. I was a mess. For the first time I was not told how dumb I was or that I was a demon in the flesh after something had happened to me. I can't remember how long I stayed home, but I know it was at least a couple of days.

My dad had a newfound interest in my wellbeing, it seemed, and I knew it was simply because I was willing to let him do whatever he wanted to me sexually. I played the part as well as I could.

On the weekends, my stepmother would leave on Saturday morning at around 10:00 a.m. and would return sometimes as late as 11:00 p.m., but never before 7:00 or 8:00. This left me caring for the children, cooking, cleaning, and seeing to the needs of everyone and everything. I was becoming a favorite with my dad and someone my stepmother utilized to her utmost ability.

She seemed almost to have a fear of being mean, because now my dad had a "reason" to like me. She was very aware of what was going on. She never spoke to me about it until years later. She spoke then about how she had been in pain over it and had been very angry at my dad, yet she had never done a thing about it, and had even lied for many years about it. She had never once tried to protect me in any way, neither as a small child nor as an adult. She had had many chances to show she cared for me, but she never did.

I know that she understood my fear of my dad, as we all feared him. So she skillfully used it to her advantage. She was able to get me to care for the children, make bread, and do dishes for a very large family, wash out diapers and do laundry. She piled on more and more, yet I seemed to be able to handle it.

I had acquired a new skill that I would use for years, that would make me tired beyond words. Even though my dad was being nice to me (of course that meant being raped by him) by not beating me or degrading me daily and calling me "demon in the flesh," I somehow felt a little hope and happiness. I know that sounds warped, but at the time, things were better than they had been.

My new skill was to keep everyone happy at all times, no matter what. What a huge order; and of course I could never acquire such a hopeless skill, but I tried. I worked hard at keeping my dad happy by doing as much work as I could, smiling and pretending everything was okay. Keeping the house as clean as possible so my dad and stepmother didn't fight, making meals for my brothers so they didn't hate my stepmother so much, caring for the younger children, cooking and cleaning so my stepmother would not get mad at me and somehow turn my dad against me. It was quite a juggling act.

There was some relief, that first summer that school was out, as sometime during that seventh grade school year, my family had found a church in Phoenix, one hundred miles from where we lived. We drove there almost every Sunday night for church service. It started about 6:00 p.m., I believe, and didn't finish until 9:00 p.m. or so. It was a Pentecostal church, full of screaming and beating of the pulpit. (I always felt very scared and guilty while going there)

57

However, it gave me a chance to be around other people and get away from my father.

My dad attended a few times to check it out and see what we were learning. In his mind, he was above churches though, and only berated us whenever we tried to attend. Even though we were a very religious family and appeared to the common person as "God fearing people," the dark underlying truth was that we were more evil than most people I have ever met since leaving my home: Sexual abuse between father and daughters and between siblings, beatings, and fear pumped in on a daily basis—not because my dad was a drunkard who flew into a drunken rage and raped me, but because he felt he had the right to do the things he did.

Instead, on the outside, we all seemed "very godly." If you don't give your life to Jesus to be born again, you will go to hell. If you drink, smoke, wear pants, makeup, and jewelry other than a wedding band or maybe a necklace, then you will go to hell. Well, at home I did very well: I played the part. I even lived in constant fear of God. My siblings and I equated our righteousness with whether or not our dad was mad at us!

I was so afraid of the return of Jesus that I would often have a panic attack at the sight of clouds in the sky, because remember *He will return in clouds of glory.*

I don't recall even a moment of rest in my soul, and as far as learning Scripture was concerned, I only read my Bible when I was in trouble or was feeling really guilty. If I tried to say something about my thoughts on what I read, I was careful to make sure it lined up with what we were taught. If you made yourself sound good enough, you would get "brownie points," such as being brought up in a conversation with someone else about how you were really growing spiritually. My dad would never pay a compliment to your face, as he said that caused pride.

Summer afforded more opportunity, not only for my dad to abuse me sexually, but also, by that time, for my brother, Sam, to work on me. He started buying me food to cook. I had started to learn to cook and decided that I could make people smile through baking and cooking. Oh, and one more thing: they would be nice to me! I needed that so badly, every day.

Laden with guilt, fear, and the feeling of filth, I fell into one more trap created for me. As my brother started buying me foods to cook, he also started trying to persuade me that I was very beautiful, and then he started buying me clothes. Then I felt I owed him, so I would do exactly what he wanted; now I had to make sure my dad didn't find out about it.

Fortunately, this was short lived, as I finally found the courage to say "no". I avoided my brother. I fell into a pattern of survival that would take me down a compromised life path for many more years.

I returned to school in 1979 for what would end up being my final year. I was thirteen and in the eighth grade. I knew it would be my last year, as all children except the three oldest were pulled out of school after the eighth grade. The law wasn't enforced after that. My dad constantly made sure we knew that if we went to school any longer, the government would "brainwash" us.

My dad made sure that he pumped fear into us as often as he could. Every idea, every belief system other than his, was wrong and of Satan. He felt he knew everything there was to know, and what *he* didn't know was just not necessary or even wrong to know about.

I was really far too scared to think on my own. I was very careful to listen and try to become what I felt I should become. After all, would my own dad, who was such a great Christian, lead me astray in any fashion? I knew that the sexual abuse made me feel very sick and very dirty, and yet through it, I received his approval. He himself said that Jesus was not concerned about *what* we were willing to do, just that we learned to be willing, to submit to whatever we were asked to do. Then we would be in Jesus' will. I tried very hard to be the person Jesus wanted me to be. I wanted my heart to be in the right place. The warping of Scripture is very hard to heal.

As my last school year progressed, I was truly feeling more and more trapped. I really liked school and the principal of the school and my school counselor several times asked me to stay in school. Both the principal and the counselor knew my dad. They also knew his policy of pulling his children out of school after the eighth grade. It was very hard for me when they would call me to the office and ask, "Please stay; you are a bright girl and you could go far." I wanted so badly to be an attorney. It was a real dream but I had to let it go.

I was still hanging around a rough group that year, and I underestimated a situation one day. Several of the kids told me about a "birthday party" for one of the girls. We would have to ditch last period, but we would be back in time to get on the bus. I remember feeling very excited, thinking that it was really a birthday party, since I had never really been to any parties since I left my sister in Oklahoma. I really didn't want to be a bad girl. I had made friends with some bad kids, but once again, they were *nice* to me. I would do anything to have someone be nice to me.

I arrived at the party a little nervous, as I had ditched class, and even though it was not the first time, I still knew it was wrong. I arrived at the house, which was not far from the school, and as I walked in the door, I realized that something was wrong. There was no cake and the smell of pot was very clear in the air. There were kids making out in different places.

Then I realized that three or four boys that I went to school with were there, all staring at me and laughing. I suddenly felt very uneasy. I knew them well enough. I really liked one of the boys, but he was dating a friend of mine. Then without warning, three of the boys got up and came across the room, grabbed me by the arms and pulled me into a room. At first, I had no idea what they were up to, but soon they were holding me down and taking my clothes off. I was mortified! I begged them to stop, I cried and struggled, but they were stronger than I was. Two of the boys raped me that day. The humiliation was horrifying.

It only ended when it did because someone yelled that the mother of whoever lived in the house was on her way home. They let me up and I dressed quickly and ran out of the house. I didn't quit running until I reached the bus stop. I hit my ankle on a rock while I was running, and it hurt badly for weeks, but of course I could not say even one word about that or the pain of being raped. After all, one of the reasons my dad said that he had sex with me was to keep me from having sex with other boys, and that it would help me stay "pure." I agreed; I always agreed, it was the only safe thing to do.

As sad and warped as I know it is, my dad believed that incest was not bad, as long as only the dad did it. He even told us that Scripture approved of this behavior. He also told us that children only think incest is wrong because the government says it is wrong. I agreed once again. I agreed with everything he said. It made me safe. I also came to believe, somewhere along the line, that if I were on my dad's good side, then I also was "right" with Jesus.

I really wanted to be right with Jesus; it was very important to me. Our family had left the church in Phoenix due to a change in that church's beliefs, so we kids found a church closer to home. It was only about twenty miles away in Prescott, Arizona. We attended quite regularly, sometimes twice a week. This was okay with my dad because he believed that the Pentecostal church was not part of the harlot church spoken of in Revelation. Later, he would lump this church into the same category because it found out about the abuse and excommunicated us when my dad and older sister refused to change.

One night I took a friend from school to our church; she was Catholic, and since I had attended church with her a couple of times (I didn't tell my dad), she decided to go with me. I went dressed up with high heels and makeup, looking somewhat wild: pretty sinful for that church and my family.

I had been allowed to spend the night with my friend, something seldom granted, but since I was a very good girl now, I had more privileges. It was a revival and the preacher was really coming down on sin. At the altar call, I went forward and so did my friend. I truly asked Jesus to cleanse me. I really, really wanted to feel clean for once in my life, just once, and that night I did.

School ended a short time later and I really tried to hang on to the feeling of purity. With school out and with no hope to return, I was stuck in Skull Valley except when we went to church. In some ways, I was happy to let go of school because I was tired of trying to lead a double life. I still wore pants under my skirt and changed on the bus.

I felt out of place most of the time, and the rape left me scared even to go to school. The boys who had raped me made fun of me, not about the rape but saying that I was dumb and stupid. They just wanted to hurt me more, after having hurt me already. I felt crazy when I was around them. I tried to avoid them, but they were in several classes with me.

I never told any adult until I told my first husband years later. I did not tell my stepmother until I was about twenty, and then she told my dad. He didn't have much to say except, "why didn't you tell us when it happened?" I just said, "I don't know," rather than tell him how scared I was of him.

Once school ended, I was left more and more with my younger siblings. I became the favorite babysitter, housekeeper, cook, and sex object. Two of my brothers still attempted, every chance they had, to get me to do sexual favors. I had become strong enough to say no, sort of. I really just tried to avoid them. Of course, my dad continued the sexual abuse.

I truly wanted to be a "proper" Christian girl and felt very righteous doing "good things" for the family. The reason I was the favorite in some ways was that I really put my whole self into cooking, cleaning, and caring for the younger and older siblings. I wanted to be all I could be so that God would love me, and I knew that would only happen if I pleased first my dad and then the rest of the family. Looking back is very hard to do sometimes, as the picture is so clear to me now that most of what I learned was wrong.

As if I weren't busy enough, I decided to start my own business. I was thirteen and just out of the eighth grade and of course I knew I wouldn't return to school. Not wanting to be broke, I started my own plant business: not very big, just a few houseplants. I learned to propagate them, and then I moved to propagating grape vines, willow trees, cottonwood trees and any other plant that I could get to root. I loved plants so very much and could hide myself in the joys of watching them grow. I also held in my heart a secret hope to be able to have money one day, real money that would provide for me and a family that I prayed I would have, a husband and children.

I worked hard at my plant nursery as often as I could. There was so much work to do and keeping everything as peaceful as possible was something I took upon myself. If I cleaned, cooked and was "very friendly" to my dad, usually I was able to keep the house fairly peaceful; that meant talking to my dad for hours sometimes, always agreeing in a way that made my dad feel better, and always trying to match my opinion to his.

I didn't understand what I was doing at the time. I just knew it seemed to keep him happy, and that was all I cared about. If he was happy, then I must be doing what God wanted. It would take me years and years to work through that mindset to heal, and truly learn the right way to handle relationships.

The summer after school ended, I turned fourteen. I was an emotional wreck most of the time but I never let it show until one day as I was dealing with one of my older brothers, who was making a very pressing sexual advance that I rejected. I fell apart. It was more than I could handle, having my dad and my brothers pawing at me, being tired from all the work, and, what was worse, trying to keep all the secrets. Even though my brothers knew my dad was abusing me sexually, I couldn't let my dad know that my brothers were pressuring me for sex. My dad still would have beaten them.

I had to act as if nothing were happening, smile, and be kind. After all, had my dad not taught us that Jesus didn't care what you submitted to, as long as you were willing? Once, shaking badly and crying, I told my stepmother I just felt like a sex object! She told me I had better shut up or she would tell my dad. I felt trapped, scared, and very alone. I pulled myself back together and tried to act as if all were okay.

When I say I never let my emotions show, it's not that I wasn't emotional; I was, but I always pretended it was about something other than what was really going on.

The church that my siblings and I attended, the church in which I had become a child of God, was now becoming a nightmare. It seems that word had gotten out that my dad was having sex with my older sister, who told everyone that it was her choice and that it was not a sin. Now, no one asked me about this; however, the pastor and deacons started acting very strange around me, and then the pastor and a friend of my dad decided to talk to my dad, who did not attend the church, and let him know that what he was doing was terribly wrong.

Well that didn't go very well. My dad made sure they both knew that he was doing nothing wrong and that they had no right confronting him. He knew God much better than either of them did, after all. My dad also told the pastor that he would understand when his daughters grew up how hard it was not to have sex with them. At that point in my life, I was truly confused. I had heard what the church had to say, but my dad was so convincing and besides, although I knew he was sexually abusing me, I didn't want the church to know it. It made me feel so dirty and sick to my stomach.

Besides all that, if my dad said it, it had to be the truth. He read the Bible and understood it better than anyone did; he was led by the Spirit, and he understood things in the Bible that organized churches didn't understand. The whole world of the church was bad and only a chosen few could ever know what he knew. Every organized church was part of the harlot church mentioned in Revelations. If I just kept reminding myself of that, then I would feel safe that I was in "God's will"!

Chapter 10
CPS

LITTLE DID I KNOW THAT ONE OF MY SISTERS, Jackie, and possibly another sister, Sue, with whom I had lived in Oklahoma, along with others, had all gone to child protective services to make a report of the abuse in my home. I started hearing a few words about it here and there but I figured all was fine. After all, there was nothing wrong with what was going on, was there? I thought more and more about it, but never too long, as it only brought unrest and an uneasy, icky feeling. I just wanted to be happy, and if I just tried very hard, I could pretend really well. After all, my dad was very happy with me.

Not all the family felt that way, especially my stepmother and my older sister Sherri. They both treated me very distantly and spent as little time around me as possible. Sherri was either in the little travel trailer she lived in or was in town all day with my stepmother. There was always discourse between the two and I didn't have time for either. My dad often "visited" Sherri in her travel trailer to "talk" to her but we all knew what was going on.

I felt very sorry for Sherri, even though she also was very hard for me to understand. It hurt and angered me to see her so pitiful; however, I had no idea at the time that she was also depressed.

My stepmother avoided me unless she needed a job done. I could tell that she almost tiptoed around me at times. I started to figure it out as my dad began to "confide" in me and tell me how bad his sex life was, and that was why he appreciated me so much. Part of me felt very happy: I had finally arrived; I had finally become someone. I could make my dad happy, so that meant that I was all right with God.

Soon my dad was berating my stepmother every chance he could, telling me how unhappy he was. I was fourteen at the time; what was I supposed to do? It made me feel so much pressure. My dad was always irritated with her, not that he had ever treated her with any respect. He treated her like a hired hand that he really didn't like.

It became very hard to pray, as to think about God, meant I had to think about the church we had been going to. Then the church made its next move and asked my sister if she would denounce the sin and say that what my dad was doing was wrong. Her response was to stand by my dad and say that it was not sin. I was never asked.

My sister Sherri was excommunicated from the church so we all had to quit going. After all, who would or could question my dad? He was the only one who could be right; he had studied the Bible and told us that God never punished Lot for his sin with his daughters and that their children were blessed by God. Wow! I learned, much later, how wrong he was and that he had truly deceived us, but at the time, I only read a few verses in the New Testament before falling asleep. I did not know the word of God or God Himself, Jesus or the Holy Spirit—I had given my life to Jesus but I had no idea what that really meant; that would come much later.

I was also taught that the law in Leviticus on sexual purity did not pertain to my dad. Leviticus 18:6 says that no one is to approach any close relative to have sexual relations. My dad's take on that was that I was not a "close relative, I was blood." It still amazes me how people will warp the word of our Lord and Savior for their own sick, perverted pleasure. At the time, however, I felt reassured in some strange way that my dad would never lead me astray because he was such a godly man.

I often felt guilt through the years that made it hard to pray unless I was broken and crying, asking for help to make it through. I didn't really know for what else to pray. Some of the guilt was from times when my dad would have pain in his chest and he would believe he was having a heart attack. This happened every now and then, and my stepmother would come to us and say, "If you want your dad to live, you had better start praying hard." Well, that might make some kids sad and start praying, but I just started thinking how wonderful my life would be. Free, free, free! I couldn't pray. I felt too happy and guilty all at the same time.

Other times I would feel the same way, such as when my dad went on a trip to Texas to see my sister Jackie, or to California to see his sister. I would spend several minutes, sometimes, putting together a traffic accident in my mind in which he died. I would feel so free thinking those thoughts. However, I quickly would feel great guilt and shame; I just wanted to be free of this man.

I'm not sure what time of day or what day of the week it was, it's all such a blur, but I heard someone saying that the sheriff was outside. There were several officers as well as other people, it was all so scary that my heart was pounding. I don't remember if I just went out there or if I was called. I wanted to pass out; the fear was enormous and paralyzing. The next thing I do remember was that I was standing outside with the people introducing themselves. I don't recall their names but I do remember hearing *child protective services*.

Finally my day had come. One might think I would now be fine, or maybe that, had it been handled right, I could have been freed sooner. Instead, after introducing themselves, they started asking me questions: Paula, has your dad ever touched you in a sexual way or had sex with you? Well, now, as for answering, I thought, "Just say yes and it will all be over." Instead, I gave a very convincing, "no, never" but of course it was the only thing I could say because my dad was standing right next to me.

Oh, if I had just been taken away from him that day, I would have spoken up, told the truth, and I would have saved my younger sisters! I wouldn't dare go against my dad, he was a very "godly man" and a very violent man who knew the word of God, and he "knew" God better than anyone. I couldn't chance it. Every officer that stood there that day knew I was lying.

Talk had become very common in our small valley about there being extensive sexual abuse in our family, but I couldn't say anything, I just couldn't; the fear was too real and I had no strength.

Child protective services also asked my dad that day if he had ever sexually touched me and, of course, he said no; then they asked to make a return visit another day to check up on me. My dad agreed and a day was set; however, I don't remember which day. I do remember that a very sinking scared, sick feeling came over me as the sheriff and the deputy left. I'm not even sure of the conversation; I just knew that I was scared.

There was always much talk about anything that happened at our home. Always talk, discussion after discussion, mostly ideas that my dad never even accomplished, because all he did was talk, talk, talk.

So believe me, my dad had to reinforce that he was doing nothing wrong and that this government had no right to come in and question us, and that if they found out and took all us kids, they would put us in horrible foster homes. It was none of their business. The terror on my dad's face was obvious to me: he knew he had a very big problem on his hands.

He became very distant and hardly talked to me until the time of the appointment with CPS. As always when anyone came, we had to clean, clean, clean and this time was certainly no exception. The kitchen was very hard to keep clean as there was always something going on in it. And the floor: well, after years of people walking on it and scrubbing it, the linoleum was worn all the way to the wood in many areas. It was very embarrassing.

My dad had bought indoor–outdoor carpet for the floor; however, it was decided it would not be put down until all the kids were gone, as they would just destroy it. I was not sure what to make of that, as he kept having more kids. It just seemed as if there were no logic to it. I started to wonder about ideas I had heard but would never have said anything about except to agree.

The day finally arrived when CPS was to come. It was summer, probably July. The trees, flowers, grass, pond, fields, and garden were all at their best. Our place was beautiful and it worked when CPS arrived—the same man and woman as the first time, only this time they came alone, with no law enforcement. They just seemed like two very nice people.

I wish I could remember that day better, but all I really remember is how long it seemed they were there. Question after question and then the words, "Well we certainly don't see a reason to return, as we feel Paula is in great hands here." "What a wonderful place you have, Mr. Sanders; we would love to come back sometime just to see your lovely place and children."

I knew it was over; my dad had worked his magic again, and he was so good at it. He lied so well. Oh, but wait, it wasn't a lie: it was only a lie if you lied to another of God's children, and if my dad didn't "feel" you were one of God's children then he could lie to you. Some of my family still holds to that belief even today.

Once again, the change was very apparent. I felt so much fear as my dad became quite cold toward me and said very little for a while. Then one day, he sat me down and told me that he was never going to touch me or any of his girls again, as he didn't want to get in trouble and maybe this was God telling him he didn't "need" to do this anymore. My dad spent plenty of time trying to justify his actions and had said many times that he just didn't understand why God put the "burden" on him to have sex with his daughters.

I became very afraid of what would happen to me without the "special" treatment that I had while my dad was sexually abusing me: What would happen to me now? This fear came from the fact that my dad treated me better than even my stepmother and my other sister. I know it was sick, and it made me feel sick, yet I fought the feeling, shoving it way down when it surfaced. I would take the feeling and say to myself that, for sure, my dad was right and there was no sin in it because he said so; just because it made me sick didn't mean it was wrong, I was just a bad girl. But now what would I do? Would he start yelling at me, calling me demon in the flesh, beating me? I didn't know, but I did know that I was scared again ... really scared, and it began to eat at me.

I tried to make some kind of life for myself, privately relieved that he wasn't coming to my room anymore, trying to touch me while I was working, feeling watched. He kept to his word and never touched me again. That built some trust in me. He seemed to be following what God had wanted, and I really wanted to believe that this man followed God. I needed that reassurance so much. It kept me safe in my very sick, scared mind.

I turned fifteen the August after CPS came. I worked very hard to continue to be a perfect daughter, cleaning, cooking, smiling, and agreeing with every conversation that my dad and I had. I needed to try to keep everything perfect; it was my only hope to prevent my dad beating me again. I learned to push every feeling I had down and never really say what I thought. In fact, I really started to believe everything this man said. It was just so much easier, and he continued to be very nice to me because I was such a "smart girl" and I agreed with his every word. I had found a new way to survive, and it seemed to work. I still seemed to be his favorite, which caused pain and suffering for many family members, but especially for my stepmother and two of my sisters, Sherri and Ellie. I was so fixated on survival that nothing else mattered. I wanted to be seen as good in Dad's eyes so I could be "in" with Jesus.

I still wet the bed and with my new situation, I even wet more, as my nerves were raw every day. The mattress I had been given after returning from Oklahoma had developed a hole in it and I worked very hard to hide it. I had learned how to care for myself out of self-preservation and fear of discovery.

Maria, who I had met in school and with whom I had gone to church, had remained my friend. I had been allowed to spend the night with her a few times. One night I went to her house, and while asleep, I started to wet the bed. I did wake up and was able to stop it and get to the bathroom. It was always my worst nightmare to have happen to me. The few times that I did spend the night at someone else's house, I rarely allowed myself to sleep for fear that I would wet the bed.

The fall of 1981 came and with it, some relief, as I knew that it wouldn't be long before I wasn't quite as busy. I had spent that summer selling my plants and many items from our very large garden at swap meets. We had planted many items and sold any extra. I worked with my brother Andy on the garden goods, as the garden was mostly his to make money from, and he helped me with my plants, loading and unloading. My brother Sam sold honey that he got from his own hives, so we had a little business and even though it was tiring, it was exciting.

I was so excited when I thought about how I was going to grow my business over time and make money. I found a great deal of joy hiding in that thought as I worked: growing, caring, packing products, loading, unloading, and selling.

I had successfully pushed down most of my fears, as it seemed that I was no longer going to be abused sexually or physically, so I started to believe, at least on the surface, that I would be okay. I still worried every minute about being right with God. But I had started to believe that I must be "okay" because my dad seemed happy with me.

I guess it all took a toll on me though, and in September of 1981, I had my first really bad illness. I had never been very sick before that time. Maybe a cold here or there, I think the stomach flu maybe once or twice but nothing serious. I didn't even get childhood vaccinations or childhood viruses. I had gone through a time of very severe stomach pains that made it difficult to walk when I was between the ages of nine and eleven; however, I was not a sick child.

My life changed with what started out to be a sore throat. At first, it hurt and I was very, very tired, so I stayed home that weekend from the swap meet, fully expecting to return the following week.

Well I was wrong, very wrong. Maybe that would have been the case if I had been taken to the doctor, but instead I was told I would be fine, and to gargle with salt and sleep. However, I was not fine after one week; I was considerably worse, to the point of not being able to sleep more than a couple of hours in a twenty-four hour period. I couldn't swallow except with much effort and most of that went up my nose. My stepmother would check on me and ask how I was doing, but there was not much to say or do.

During the day, I would try to find a warm sunny place in a window and possibly sleep for a few minutes. I was in so much pain and so weak I could hardly stand, and eating was out of the question: food wouldn't go down my throat because it was too swollen. I couldn't even open my mouth because it was so swollen, even on the outside of my neck.

I felt my dad tried to ignore me by staying away, but one day he came to me after I had been sick for about four weeks and said to me that if I would just get up and have a merry heart, I would get better. I just needed to start doing something; after all, he had had sore throats as a child that were just as bad, and he had just kept going.

Well, I can remember thinking: I'm sure he was just as sick, and so I'll do what he says and get better. After all, he was always right.

So, in pain and so weak I could barely stand, I went to the kitchen and tried sweeping the floor. Without me cooking, cleaning, and being the second mom (or actually the first mom), things had seriously deteriorated.

The house was filthy and I felt overwhelmed just walking around in it, but I was also too weak and in too much pain to do anything about it. However, this day I would get better if I just did as he said. So, I continued to sweep the floor, fighting against passing out from the weakness.

I hadn't eaten solid food for nearly four weeks at that point, and I had lost twenty pounds. Thirst plagued me so much that what I dreamed of during the few minutes I slept was about drinking water, which I suppose made me swallow and I would wake with a horrible pain in my throat and ears. I couldn't watch another person drink anything as it made me almost crazy because I was so thirsty.

Sometimes I only urinated once every two days. I tried so hard to sweep that floor and be happy but I couldn't even hold myself upright and I realized it was pointless. I had to lie down or I would fall. As I walked to the little pallet I had made where I could get some sun, I felt an overwhelming sense of despair. It was no use and for the first time since it all began, I wanted to die.

That night after everyone had gone to bed, I went to the kitchen and started my routine of trying to eat and drink something. I had given up on trying during the day, as no one wanted to look at me. I looked like death. I made something hot to drink and tried to drink it. I worked at it very hard, swallowing very small sips, and got about four ounces down. The rest of it just came back up my nose. It completely exhausted me to try to drink anything. I also would try to drink some beef broth and would get down a small amount. Sometimes, out of hunger, I would tell myself I was just going to make myself some oatmeal and eat it. So, I would make it and then remember I couldn't even open my mouth to put it in and would have to just leave it.

Some days, though, I didn't feel any hunger at all, just thirst, horrible thirst. I became so weak that I could hardly get up and some days only got off the couch maybe once during the day to use the bathroom.

It was getting very cold by now outside. We had an indoor toilet but we were not allowed to use it. We had to go out to the outhouse, and it was so cold that I knew I couldn't make it. So I would use a can and then try to get enough energy to take it out. Because it was too painful to swallow and my saliva was very thick, I spit it out in a cup, and at night, I would try to clean these out. I do believe my stepmother tried to show some compassion for me at times and took out my urine can and spit cup when I just couldn't get up.

By November, there was not much left of me. I had lost about twenty-eight pounds and I was nothing but skin and bones. I was so weak that even my dad seemed to be a bit worried. He didn't come around me much, no one did. I was very alone. I prayed so much, asking God to help me, please. I was sure that it was because I was a bad person that this was happening to me. However, my dad didn't tell me I was, he just never tried to help me, such as take me to the doctor or get any medical attention at all.

Then one day he came into my room, sat on a chair, and said to me that as soon as I got well he was going to build me a greenhouse. I guess he knew that I loved my plants and that maybe it would make me happy and I would get better. Well, I'm not sure if it did or not, but I did start finally to improve very slowly. My dad always said that God had told him to offer me the greenhouse, and so he believed that was what made me well. I agreed, even though I thought he was wrong. I would have agreed, anyway, if it made me feel right with God.

Thanksgiving came and went, and by the second week of December, most of the pain in my throat had gone away and I was slowly able to drink again. Oh, it was so wonderful to not be thirsty!. It took me another six months to return somewhat to normal, but this would start a pattern of sickness that would continue for years to come. Actually, I would never be the same.

The following spring I started selling what I had in my nursery: bare root strawberry plants, asparagus, red raspberries, to name a few. I loved it. I worked very hard and kept dreaming that one day I would have my own place.

I still worked very hard to please my dad and to keep everything just as right as possible. I tired easily though, and needed many naps; without them I couldn't function. I had to be careful if I extended myself at all. My body hurt most of the time, especially my legs. At the swap meet that year, I met a boy and I thought I was in love. He wanted me to run away with him to Hawaii, but of course, I would not have done that. I was far too scared. I would need my dad's approval for God to approve. I avoided that mistake not because I knew what was right or wrong, but strictly out of fear.

I had turned sixteen that summer and was very confused about life. I didn't know how to make decisions based on good principles, I just knew that if Dad approved, then God approved.

I prayed but always with the feeling and belief that, if my dad thought it was a good thing, then it had to be. It felt fearful and sickening at times but it was also in a strange way the only "safe" way to get an answer.

Mark moved to Hawaii and life moved on. September came that year and I got sick again with my throat ailment. This time it only lasted a couple of weeks, and I was so thankful.

My plant nursery sales slowed down during fall, but my home responsibilities were always there. I picked up every responsibility I could to keep peace in the home, and I talked to my dad almost daily.

During our conversations he would say things that I wouldn't quite understand sometimes, like, I wish your sister Ellie or your sister Sherri were more like you. I wish to this day that I could have understood him at that time, but I would be an adult before I did. It bothered me that he said these things, yet I also felt somewhat good: He wasn't sexually abusing me anymore, and I had successfully avoided being beaten and called a demon in the flesh or other cruel things. Instead, he now praised me. I had reached quite a level with him, and he also told me how intelligent I was. Wow! What an ego boost. I didn't feel it was an ego boost, I just felt it bought me dad and God points.

I dreamed often of a husband, as I just knew that if I had a husband then everything would be okay.

But while I waited, there was some fun that entered our life. Someone had invited my brothers to go roller-skating. My brothers were now adults and worked various jobs as well as their small business, so there was a little extra money. At first, my dad wasn't very excited about us doing this, but if we completed the many chores first, we could go skating. It was the best thing in the world for me. I loved it! So did my brothers and my sister Ellie. On Friday or Saturday nights, we went skating. I never tried so hard at anything. I fell far more in the beginning than anyone I knew. My balance for that sort of thing was learned slowly. I had no confidence.

Even learning to ride a bike had taken until I was nine because I had been so scared. I bruised myself badly on my elbows, knees, and sides (I wanted to learn to turn around and skate backwards), but I wouldn't give up. I was never a great skater, but I did do pretty well considering that most of my time while skating was spent worrying whether or not my stepmom was taking care of her kids and the house.

My siblings would get very angry with me, as I would obsess about making sure everything was done: dinner fixed, house in order, bread baked, enough wood cut for the stove, laundry done, dry laundry brought in. I had to obsess; if I didn't do this, all hell could break loose. My step mom wasn't going to make sure these things were taken care of, and she would make sure to point out that Paula had not completed her jobs before leaving.

I wasn't terribly worried on the upper level of my mind that I would be beaten; it had become almost worse than that. I worried that my dad would start yelling and saying horrible things to everyone and hitting other younger brothers and sisters, and also yelling and screaming at my step mom.

It's not that I felt so much love for her, because I don't think those feelings ever had a chance to grow; it was more that I couldn't handle any anger, yelling, and hitting. My nerves would just fall apart, and the fear was so debilitating that I would tremble inside for days. Then, of course, I knew God was mad at me also for not making sure everything was perfect! It had to be, if at all possible. Nothing hurt me more than to see any of my siblings beaten or to hear horrible things said. I just felt a rage inside that I can't even put into words. But I would never say anything to my dad, never! I would have been going against God's will.

The responsibility I felt was far beyond normal, but it was survival at its worst and I didn't see any way around it. I tried daily to convince myself it was what God wanted and therefore God was happy with me.

Chapter 11
I'm in Love

JANUARY 1981 WAS THE BEGINNING OF THE END of all my problems, or so I thought. I was still living the dream of having a husband that I could treat like a king, unlike my stepmother, and in return he would love and cherish me and we would forever be happy.

I had long daydreams as I did my daily chores of cleaning, baking, and keeping the fire going in the kitchen so that the house would stay warm, about how I would do all these duties for my husband and if I did, then it would all be perfect.

I didn't really think much about having a baby; I wasn't even sure if I wanted one. There was never a great longing to have a baby except with the distant thought about how I would never spank or hurt my child in any way for wetting the bed. I was very sure. I had so many younger brothers and sisters that I guess I never really thought about having a child. I was only sixteen although it was very much expressed and taught in our home that having children was the only thing God expected us to do, and it was the only way to receive jewels in our eternal crown when we reached heaven. With that teaching, I knew that it was something I should just do.

I received a call one day in January from my friend Maria whom I had known from school. We had kept in contact on and off. She was very excited talking about the young man she was dating, and how much they were in love. She explained how her boyfriend had a friend who was looking for a date and wanted to know how I felt about a blind date.

Well, I finally got up the nerve to ask my dad if I could go, but not before working very hard to make sure everything was done. Heart pounding, I approached my dad and told him about the young man that wanted to go out with me on a blind date. I wasn't sure of the look in my dad's eyes, I just couldn't read him, but I hoped beyond hope that he would say yes. He looked at me for a while and then said to me, "Only if I meet him first."

So I called Maria and told her the stipulation, and it was set up for all three to come the twenty miles to Skull Valley so my dad could meet this young man. They were expected to arrive by 5:00 p.m. When I saw their truck pull up outside I was scared to death. I went to the door and welcomed them in. I was horrified; here stood my beautiful friend Maria and her boyfriend, tall nice looking and clean. Then there stood my future date, overweight, with sloppy, filthy clothes, unshaven and with a baseball cap on. There was an exchange of names (his was Chris) and I could smell alcohol on all their breaths, along with cigarette smoke on my future date. With my heart sinking in my chest, I really just wanted this to be over. They stayed just long enough to explain that Chris was so unkempt because he had been out cutting wood. After they left, I told my dad that I was not going out with him and of course, he agreed.

The next day, however, Maria called and with her usual excitement asked if I was going out that Friday night, January19. At first I said no, but then she begged me and promised that it would only be one time, so I agreed. So then, I had to get my dad to agree. He simply said to me, well if you want to, I guess you can go. With that, I was rather excited. I had never been out before; even my first boyfriend

I saw only at the swap meet on weekends. But this was my first date, and according to Maria, he had said I was cute and he wanted to date me. So the wheels started turning that maybe, just maybe, this was okay.

Friday night came and I dressed as specially as I could. I had very few clothes, although I was allowed to wear pants now when I went skating, but this night I just put them on and wore them. I was so jittery inside that when Chris, Maria, and her boyfriend arrived, I didn't even think. I had arranged to spend the weekend with Maria—a very rare occasion—and I was truly excited just to have a little freedom. I was even able to put down the feeling that I was leaving my stepmother with too much to take care of with her seven children. I didn't even care what this guy looked like at the moment; for once I was going out and on my first date.

When they arrived, my dad was resting upstairs so I went outside and got into the truck, a very nice new black Ford that was the envy of all who saw it. And Chris, well, he was much cleaner than the first time, still overweight but cleaner and dressed somewhat better, and he smelled really nice. The four of us rode in the front seat of that truck. It was so crowded that I was pushed up right next to Chris and he could barely shift gears. We went to dinner, and as we settled in, he took a look at my salad and asked why there were bread crumbs on it. Maria explained they were croutons. Then he made funny comments for the whole evening, making us all laugh.

By the end of the night, I was starting down a very dangerous road and didn't even know it. As I looked at Chris, I started changing his outward appearance: I cut his hair, had him lose thirty pounds, put a nice western shirt and wranglers on him, and trimmed his mustache. Like that, he would do just fine. I'd have to make sure he didn't smoke anymore, even though Maria told me that she had already told him I didn't like smoking or drinking. He had said, "That's it. I won't anymore," and that was that, or so I thought.

I was so eager to please a man because I had been taught that that was my highest calling, along with having children. I also had two secrets that plagued me almost daily that I knew I would have to tell a man. One was that I wet the bed—and I felt that alone made me totally unworthy of a good man—and the other was the sexual abuse that made me feel, well, there really weren't words for it, as I truly wanted to believe that it was okay. After all, that's what my dad said the Bible said, but somehow when I thought about telling another person, especially my boyfriend, I knew it was terribly wrong! So with these things to deal with, I had to just take what I got and clean the person up to make him what I wanted. What a sad way to start, but that is exactly what happened.

The next day after going out that Friday night, Maria wanted me to go over to her boyfriend's house with her, so I did, and a short time later Chris showed up. We all spent the day together. I was really trying to figure out how I felt, but I was really taken with how much this guy liked me, so I just let the day happen.

The next day was Sunday, and I called home to let my parents know I would be home that day. I'll never forget my stepmother informing me that I was in big trouble and had better get home quickly. I was in trouble for leaving without saying good-bye, but I had thought my dad was sleeping. No one ever woke him up if they knew what was best for them. My heart was racing as she told me that if we didn't come home very quickly, Chris would not be able to see me again.

We left Prescott and I told Chris that he didn't have to go and see my dad and that I was afraid for him, but he insisted. However, he didn't know my dad and how cruel he could be. So, in blind faith he walked in and sat down. He tried to explain while my dad stared him down, and to this day, because I was so scared, I can't remember everything he said, just that Chris's chin started to quiver. Then my dad finally told us that Chris could take me out again. Chris never really got over that night. It troubled him so much that he told me that he made a deal with God that night that if He made sure we would stay together, he would do whatever He wanted.

Chris and I became inseparable. He called or came to see me daily. I was in love. I dreamed of how I was going to treat him and started right away. If he came to see me, I cooked and waited on him. I met his parents, and although they seemed nice, they also didn't seem to care for me being there.

Chris and I started dating January 19 and went out at least once a week. I was never asked what was going on or if I was really going to the movies or to the skating rink. That was what Chris would tell my parents and then he would take me out in the woods for sex. I was all too willing as this meant he liked me and all that mattered was how he felt, right? I had never been to see a movie in my life. I really wanted to go, but he didn't like doing that, so I did what he wanted. I didn't even know what to want, though, for myself. I had never been anywhere so I really didn't think I was missing anything. After all, what mattered was that Chris was happy.

I was so in love, or so I thought, that when I missed my period the first week of April 1982, I didn't think much about it. But a week later when I was vomiting, I knew something was wrong and went to my stepmother. I told her about my worries. I had already told Chris, and he had bought the test. Within seconds, I knew that my life was changing, but I was too scared to let it really sink in. I wasn't sure how to tell my dad; it scared me to death. However, I did go and tell him. He just sat there for a long time and then said to me, "Do you want to marry Chris?—because I won't make you."

Well, at the time, I was so in love with the idea of being in love and wanting to get away, I would have never said I didn't want to. Besides, up to this point, for three whole, long months, Chris had been so wonderful. I just knew that everything would be perfect; I was going to be a good wife, the one who makes the marriage work. I had come to believe with my whole heart that if I were a good wife, I could make every dream of mine come true. It didn't matter that we had nothing; we had no place to live, no money, and no education. But we had love.

The morning of April 24, 1982, Chris, and I loaded up, with my dad and stepmother, in Chris's really nice truck and drove off to Las Vegas, Nevada, to get married. I was so sick on that trip I could hardly see straight. It was a strange trip. There was not much said and I really didn't care. Nausea had taken over every sense. I don't think I felt much that day, just somewhat numb. I knew this was just the way things were supposed to go because I had been told that weddings were just a waste of good money, and that going to Las Vegas was the smart and healthy thing to do. We arrived in Las Vegas and, after finding a bathroom, we located the courthouse, signed paperwork, walked into a small room, and waited for our turn.

After a few moments, a man called us in, summoned us toward his desk, asked for the money (I believe it was forty dollars), opened a drawer below him, swept the money into it, and as he did so, he closed his eyes and started reciting our wedding vows. I didn't like it at all; it made me feel, well, somewhat sad, but I quickly pushed that feeling away. I was there to be married to the man of my dreams. It would all be okay. I had plans to create a wonderful marriage. I would just do everything right. I would cook, clean, and well, I wasn't sure, but I would make it work.

We arrived back at my parent's house, the only place we had to live. We were given a room that used to be my sister's and mine when we were younger. The walls still had old bloodstains from the years that bed bugs had tormented us. I went to school every day for several years with bites all over me. The sight was sickening for me, I was so embarrassed for my new husband to see it, but somehow he didn't seem to mind; all he seemed to care about was the mattress that was on the floor: just a mattress and box spring, no frame. I just fell on the bed sick as I could be and fell asleep.

It was a very hard start but I was happy—at least I thought I was. Each day was very hard as I spent most of it being so sick that it was hard to be around anything or anyone. For four months, everything I ate came up and the smell of my husband's clothes from the tire shop was more than I could bear. I cried at the drop of a hat. I was weak and needed sleep, yet my stepmother asked, almost daily, what I was making for breakfast, lunch, and dinner. I was becoming completely overwhelmed. I finally went to my dad, and he told her not to ask me to help so much.

As my body changed, I often thought about the life growing inside of me. I enjoyed the first movement at about four months: at least I knew that the morning, noon, and night sicknesses were for a reason.

One night, exhausted, I went to bed and fell asleep very quickly. I had been married about four or five months by then. As always, I wasn't aware when it happened, but I woke up to Chris telling me that I had just wet the bed. I woke up quickly, and as I realized the fact, I felt the most horrible fear, embarrassment, and shame I had ever known since the towel that I had to wear to school in the fourth grade. It all washed over me and I fell apart. I cried so long I don't remember when I quit. I do remember Chris telling me not to worry about it. It was not a big deal. Maybe the baby had lain on my bladder wrong. I knew better, but I tried to accept his kindness. I never wet the bed after that. However, I worried about it for a long time to come.

I turned seventeen in August that year. My baby was due December 18. As I awaited the arrival of my baby, I often had very strange, sad emotions that I couldn't explain. The morning sickness had all but stopped, and I started gaining weight rapidly.

I was so hungry, and I had never had many restaurant foods before, except when I was in Oklahoma. Chris took me every Friday to eat Mexican food and then to his parents at least once or twice a week, and there was nothing but fattening food everywhere. I gained sixty pounds in four months. I was so naive about my body.

We did have a midwife we were friends with, and I went to her a couple of times to just see if she thought everything was all right.

But in my family, if you truly trusted God you didn't need to do that. You just waited and hoped everything worked out.

The midwife gave me some good information, and then I went home to wait.

Two weeks before my baby was to be born, my dad and stepmother left and went to California. So I was left with all my siblings to care for. I was so tired and very overwhelmed as I cooked and cleaned. I wanted so much for someone to help me. I was more worried than ever about having a baby. I had no idea what to expect. I had gotten to the point where I just wanted to have the baby. I had picked out a name for the baby, and even though I had picked out a boy's name, I just knew I was having a girl.

The morning of December 18, I cried. I was due that day, my parents were not home yet, and I knew the baby would be here at any time.

Chris never played much of a role in anything and was, for the most part, just there. If I asked for help, he would help, but for the most part, no matter what, I had to ask. I tried to tell if he was excited about the baby, but he didn't show very much emotion. I was fine with that, in a way. At least that's what I told myself.

I had decided to go for a two-mile walk that afternoon, and my older sister Sherri (who was the one who had helped with the diaper in the fourth grade), walked with me. I told her how tired I was and that I couldn't keep taking care of all the children by myself. I was just too tired. She told me that I needed to save my energy to have the baby and seemed very nice.

We didn't have much of a relationship; however, I knew she was the one that was going to help deliver my baby because there was no one else.

Then it hit me—the pains were getting closer together. I realized it a few hours after my long walk, and also, unfortunately, after eating about twenty chocolate candies while wrapping Christmas presents for Chris's family.

Chris's family didn't know what to make of the family their son had gotten himself into, and while his younger sister and mother were always good to me; his dad really wasn't good to me at all. In fact, he truly had a hate for me and he showed it every chance he got. He made comments just to see if he could hurt me, and he seemed to enjoy it. It seems that Chris's parents had had a dream that their son would never marry and instead would stay and take care of them. Well, I messed that up, and his dad wanted me to pay. He would get his first and his best jab at me very shortly after my precious little Amanda Annette was born.

As the night of December 18 wore on, I realized at about 8:30 p.m. that I was in labor, and my sister and Chris started putting everything in order for a baby to be born. It seemed straight out of the early century: some boiling water, string, scissors, disinfectant, and plastic. Very crude and old fashioned, but this was how we did it.

As the contractions grew closer and more painful, I felt fatigue set in, then vomiting. Remember the chocolate candies?—Well I did and it took years before I could even look at one again.

I didn't expect that having a baby could be so painful. I worked at keeping a cool head and prayed. I was truly begging for this to be over. I was so tired, cold, shaking, and vomiting. And of course it was over shortly into the nineteenth of December, 1982; Amanda was born. She was so beautiful, with a full head of dark hair. She looked so much like Chris. I was shocked.

All the babies in our family were born with light hair or no hair, but this little wonderful, beautiful seven-pound, five-ounce, perfect baby was olive skinned with a full head of hair. Chris was half-Italian, and Amanda had received the Italian half. I held her and wondered what to do. I had helped care for so many siblings but this was different: this one was mine and she needed to be fed. I had to nurse her. I worked hard at it but I was in so much pain I couldn't think, I had done it, I had given birth, but now the pain overwhelmed me.

We never took anything for pain, natural or otherwise. We were taught that pain was just something God wanted us to have because it taught us to be the people we needed to be. It would take me a long time to heal.

The first night, or what was left of it, passed and morning came. I tried to hold Amanda and nurse her. She was so little but everything about her seemed perfect and I felt so blessed. Sometime over the course of December 19, my parents finally came home, and I remember being glad that someone was there for the kids. I still felt guilty if I couldn't take care of them, as if they were my first responsibility and Amanda and Chris were second.

I just couldn't get over the feeling that I needed to make sure all was well in my house, actually my parent's house. By December 20, I had moved out to the living room area, as it was very cold in my room and I couldn't keep myself warm enough, or keep Amanda warm enough. So there I was, out where all could see me.

I was miserable, but I just kept telling myself it was going to be all right. Later that evening, I had Amanda laying on the hide-a-bed next to me and had the same strange feeling come over me as I had had while pregnant; one of being very lonely and sad.

But this time, there was also a strange feeling that Amanda was going away, maybe growing up too fast. Although I wasn't sure why, I started to cry and it felt awful. I prayed out of fear, not really knowing what to say or do. I just wanted to be happy, but instead I felt scared.

I knew that on December 23 we were to be out at Chris's family's house, so I forced myself out of bed, showered, got dressed, dressed Amanda, and packed for her.

We loaded Amanda into our little truck and went to Chris's family's house in Prescott. It was cold and threatened to snow, and I couldn't wait to get to his mom and dad's house. They had not seen Amanda yet, and I knew that his mother would be delighted, as indeed she was. She took Amanda and held her with the adoring look a grandmother gives. She had bought pajamas for her and after bathing her, we put a pair on her. Amanda was so pretty, her very dark hair and olive skin looked wonderful with her yellow pajamas. My heart was so full of love and awe.

I was very tired, so my mother-in-law told me to rest, saying that she would care for Amanda. As much as I wanted to just stay up and enjoy my baby, I realized I needed rest. I lay down around 10:00 p.m. and went right to sleep.

I woke when my mother-in-law came in my room with Amanda, who was crying a very fussy cry. She asked me if I would try feeding her. I wiped the sleep from my eyes, propped myself up in bed and realized it was about 2:00 a.m. I took Amanda and tried to nurse her; my milk had finally come in earlier that day and I was so glad to be able to feed her. However, she seemed very fussy and wanted nothing to do with eating, so I laid her on my chest and gently patted her back.

She started making what I thought was a contented sighing sound as she drifted off to sleep and I dozed. Ten or fifteen minutes later, I awoke and decided to move her from my chest so I could lay down, and as I picked her up I could see in the dim light that she didn't look right —she looked as if she were not breathing. I felt for her breath and realized that she wasn't.

I tried to stay calm as I called to Chris. I remember saying, "Chris wake up, Amanda's not breathing." He came out of that bed and took her away to his parent's room. I started shaking as he laid her on his parent's bed, unzipped the pajamas, and started CPR. I could see purple in the sternum area and I realized she was gone.

Chris's parents took her, wrapped her in her baby blanket, and started for the hospital seven miles away in several inches of snow. Chris and I quickly pulled ourselves together, tried to reassure his younger sister, who was crying, and also headed for the hospital. I was so scared and shaking violently; I felt totally out of control.

How could this be happening? It's not real; she will be okay; maybe the doctors can help her. Please Jesus, please, she is the only happy thing other than my husband that has ever happened to me. Please, please, please.

We arrived at the hospital and, numb with fear, I went through the doors. Someone guided me to where doctors were working on her. I was not allowed in the room but the sound coming from the room was of a ventilator, and I told them, please don't keep doing that if she is dead.

My sweet mother-in-law was gray from the grief. She had made the mistake of uncovering her when they had arrived at the hospital, and seeing the little grandbaby, who she had just met only hours before with such joy, and who was now torn from her.

In my fog, I walked to a pay phone and called my family. I'm not sure who answered the phone, but as I relayed the message that Amanda was gone, gone to heaven, I tried to sound strong; why, I cannot say.

We left the hospital empty, scared, sad, confused, and lost. Numbness set in for a while, and then all the other feelings came.

When we arrived back at my in-law's, we all went inside. It was the early morning of December 24, a time most would celebrate. The Christmas tree seemed almost wrong. There was no joy, just pain, overwhelming pain. Why, why did this happen? I would ask myself this and condemn myself many times over the next several years.

Chris sat down on the end of the bed in our room and I in a chair, and he started to cry, which broke my heart. Chris's dad walked in, sat down next to him, and tried to console him. Then he said words that would cut me so deeply that it would take years to forgive and heal from. He told Chris that he shouldn't cry because Amanda wasn't his anyway, that she belonged to someone else and that he didn't have to stay with me now if he didn't want to.

I thought I was going to die. Chris looked at his dad and told him he was wrong, but that was all he said.

I didn't know what to do or how to deal with the pain, but at that time I felt Jesus had to be angry with me. Why else would this happen to me.

Christmas day was so painful—how do you even begin to try and pretend it's okay. My mother-in-law could barely move, her heart was broken; my father-in-law didn't say much to me. I'm sure he knew I couldn't even bear to look at him.

We stayed until the day after Christmas then went home to my family. My younger sister, Ellie, was so sad. There was a silence about our home; no one knew what to say. I had bought all the items necessary for a baby, but when I arrived home, my bedroom was empty of everything that had pertained to my Amanda. I was so lost and in pain. I needed to breast feed but there was no baby, and even at seventeen, I was very naive about all of the things that could be done to help with the pain. I just suffered in silence.

The funeral was set up, I understand, between Chris's and my family. I really wasn't aware; I just knew that on the twenty-eighth day of December, after the autopsy was done, we laid our precious little girl to rest.

Chris and I were allowed to go in and sit with her for a while before the funeral. I just tried to let all the pain and confusion out. I cried out to God, but I had been told I didn't have a right to ask why, so I never did; I just tried to be a good girl and accept what had happened as God's will. That did not change how I hurt, and I cried and cried and cried. The loneliness was so overwhelming.

I did not find out what truly happened to my baby then; However, fifteen years later, I was told that it was an infection in her umbilical cord. I did not understand that at all, because I never noticed anything unusual with her umbilical cord. But a very close friend and reliable source told me that that was the reading. I never received a death certificate for her, and if one came in the mail, it was kept from me.

I was sure the sun would never shine again in my life. Amanda had been my short ray of sunshine. I even buried her in yellow. It was beautiful on her. But she was gone, and I had to try and live again. How, I had no idea, and it was a long and painful process.

Amanda would not be my only child. God had a plan to bless me in a very beautiful way, and eighteen months later to the day, I gave birth to my oldest son, beautiful and healthy.

However, I lived in a perpetual state of fear that I would lose him also. We now lived in a ten-by-fifty foot, two-bedroom one-bath mobile home. I could have put William in his own room, but I just couldn't bring myself to for many months.

When William was three months old, I became so tired and fatigued that while holding him on the edge of the bed one night, I fell asleep and fell off the bed—down went William and I. Wow! What a scared mommy and baby. We both cried. I couldn't figure out what was wrong but when I started vomiting a couple of days later—oh, I knew that feeling. Yes, I was pregnant. A month later, Chris and I moved with his job to a small town outside of Phoenix, Arizona. I had only ever lived off our property for one year when I was eleven; now I was nineteen. It was both scary and exciting.

We lived in a small apartment. We had only been there a short time when I woke up with a sore throat one morning and I felt pure dread, as I knew it was a very bad sign. It quickly progressed, and within a day, I could not swallow without it coming out of my nose.

I knew I was in big trouble. I was so thirsty that by the third day I felt I would lose my mind. It was February and very cold even for the area I lived in. I couldn't sleep. Caring for William was almost more than I could do, and the lack of food and water was more than I could handle. I just knew I had to get help. Chris put me in the truck and took me to the closest hospital. The look on the doctors' faces said it all.

They let me know that if I didn't get help very quickly, both my baby and I would die. I needed to go to a county hospital because I didn't have insurance. I was full of fear but even so, I just knew God was mad at me for going to a doctor. Only God should be healing me; Where was my faith? What was wrong with me?

But then, something very small but strong happened in me. After a six-hour wait at the county hospital in Phoenix, I finally was taken to a room. As I was being examined I realized that the people all seemed to truly care; I was reminded of the broken collar bone when I lived with my sister. Twice now, doctors had helped and showed great kindness.

After prying my mouth open and looking, the doctor told me I was very fortunate to be alive but that I would need to have surgery in the morning to clean the abscess out.

I was in so much pain and fear, but I knew that they meant well. I was put in a room and given an IV to replace the fluids.

The worst part was that the doctor told me, had I waited twenty-four more hours, my baby would have died for sure. I still remember the IV for the fluids and antibiotics as I waited, my lips cracked and my heart racing. My throat seemed to swell even more with the fluids, and then I coughed and the abscess burst. I started choking and the kindest nurse tried to help; it was the most horrible taste I had ever known. I was sure I would die. The doctor came in and checked me to make sure I had not aspirated—I hadn't, so that was good news—and then he told me that I would not need surgery but would need to stay for a few days. A short time later, I fell into a deep sleep, one that I fought to wake up from.

For the next two days, I only woke up to receive medicine and to try to eat. The relief was wonderful, and for a brief time I really felt maybe God wasn't so mad at me. God had also provided the kindest nurse one could ask for. Her presence made me feel loved. I really couldn't explain it, but she cared for me. I would wake up to her holding my hand and putting balm on my lips. She would smile so kindly and tell me I was going to be okay. I recovered quickly and went back to our apartment. I felt sickened, however, when we found out that Chris's job was over, and that we had to go back to Skull Valley.

Shortly after arriving, I realized something was terribly wrong. No one would talk to me, and if someone tried, it was very short and no one wanted to look me in the eye. Very shortly, I learned the problem was that most of the family had decided I was wrong for going to the doctor.

Then one of my brothers came to me and in a very religious voice told me that it would have been better had I died because then God could have taught my husband something. I was devastated and deep inside me something started to grow, but it was still so small even I was hardly aware of it. But once in a while I started letting my mind wonder, just a bit.

Aaron was born one year and four days after William, and I was thrilled. I continued to have some problems throughout the rest of the pregnancy, but shortly after Aaron was born, I seemed to feel better. Aaron was an easy baby to care for, compared to William, so I tried to do more.

Well I really tried to get back into good graces with my family. I was still feeling upset and confused about my brother's words, that it would have been better had I died, and I knew, by then, that the only way I could get things right with God was to have them right with my family. I had become very good at pretending, and so I pretended and even convinced myself that I wanted to make dinner for different family members and have them over as often as possible. I did that for about three months. I became very tired, but I just kept going. I was so tired, I couldn't even nurse properly, but I had to keep them happy.

In August, Aaron was almost two months old, and one of my sisters-in-law that I adored was due to have her second child. I was very excited but also felt quite nervous. She was a brittle juvenile diabetic. She wasn't supposed to even have children, and yet one of my older sisters and my brother (the one who had told me it would have been better had I died) was going to help her have her baby. I didn't know much of anything about diabetes or childbearing at that point in my life, but I soon learned that Amber was brainwashed to believe that if she really loved Jesus, she would have to quit taking insulin before the baby was born. If she didn't, Jesus wouldn't bless her.

Amber really wanted to be in the will of God, so she quit taking her insulin. As she started into labor, she had a heart attack and died. Both she and her full term son died. I was devastated and I felt the anger growing even stronger. I tried to voice my opinion, but it was pretty much drowned out by all the emotions of losing Amber and the baby. As always with my family, everyone talked and tried to turn the whole situation into some very mysterious, religious, God thing. It made me sick.

In September, Aaron was three months old; I was exhausted trying to make everyone happy and the pain in my own heart for Amber was just too much. My milk dried up and within a week, I had strep throat again. I tried for a week just to wish it away, but I just got sicker and sicker, so we found a throat doctor in Prescott and he lanced the abscess that had formed again, and I started antibiotics once more.

When I went back home, my brother, Andy, wouldn't talk to me again, but I told myself I didn't care. My dad said he would just have to leave it up to me, but that I was just making things worse in the long run. I got better for a short time but then once again became sick, and for the next nine months was sick more often than not.

I was so sick that my sister-in-law cared for Aaron nearly every day. I tried to care for William but needed help with him many days also. I felt my life was over. I couldn't do anything; the exhaustion and the constant strep with abscesses were overwhelming. It cost one hundred dollars every time I went to the doctor to have the abscess lanced. Chris was very impatient with that. I went many times that year to have vials of puss drawn out of my tonsils. It was a nightmare, and we couldn't afford it.

That was a very long winter but by June, just in time for William's first and Aaron's second birthdays, I started to feel much better. My heart was broken, though, as Aaron had built a bond with my sister-in-law to the point of calling her mom, and that hurt. It could have hurt more, but I loved Sandy very much. She couldn't have children so it was a very special time for her, but when the time came that I was well enough to have him stay home every day, it was also very hard for her.

By the end of June, shortly after William's and Aaron's birthdays, I found out I was pregnant again. I tried not to worry about the possibility of getting sick again. Morning sickness was, as always, very tough. I just tried to stay home, care for the older boys, and make it through again.

My dad decided to bring another man into the plant nursery business. I wasn't sure what to think, but I did know that I felt I was losing control of something I had wanted to be just my husband's and my own. I was too afraid to say no, as this was my dad's friend, and he had decided that he wanted to do something different with his life.

Well, the plants started arriving, the work needed to be done, and after the first week his back began to hurt; that was it, he stepped out. There was no contract that I knew of. I was very uneducated in these matters so I really didn't know what to do. I was relieved in one way but frustrated in another as now there was so much work to do and not enough help.

Chris was no help at all, he never would talk or say what he thought, and he just tried to ignore my dad as he continued to control our business; he just hoped the problems would go away. I started feeling more and more overwhelmed and angry. I couldn't understand why I had no say in my own nursery. Then one of my older brothers became a part of the company because my dad said it was for the best. I tried to be a good Christian girl who just gave everything to Jesus and believed all would be okay. However, there was a brewing in my heart that wouldn't quite go away.

I gave birth to Robert on March 29, 1987. He was another display of God's grace and mercy. After four hours of intermittent pain and about thirty minutes before he was born, I realized that I was, indeed, in labor. I woke my husband and shortly afterward, at approximately 4:30 a.m., Robert was born. We saw that he had the umbilical cord wrapped around his neck three times. Chris quickly took the cord from around his neck and then the baby started to cry. I was so shaken from the whole thing that I hardly realized this wasn't the girl I thought I was having, but instead another boy, and this one really had very boyish features; he would have made a very ugly girl.

His eyes were swollen and black and blue for several days after birth, and he probably should have been taken to a doctor, but that was still something that I couldn't bring myself to do. I still believed that it was just plain wrong to see a doctor for something so natural as having a baby. Robert was very sickly with colds and ear infections for the first couple of years of his life. I always felt it had to do with my poor health.

Chapter 12
But You Promised

I WORKED THE PLANT NURSERY EVERY DAY as soon as I had recovered enough from the birth of Robert to get back out there. With Robert in a stroller and William and Aaron running around, I potted, trimmed, and sold plants. I loved it. It was wonderful, and I really felt that this business was going to fly. The excitement was what I lived on, and I tried to ignore the fact that there was a very icky feeling that continued to rise within me.

I started to notice more and more that my dad was saying things like, "I wish your sister were more like you." At first, I thought he meant that I was a people person, and that I was compliant, married, a mother; everything he approved of.

But Ellie, well, she appeared angry. She kept leaving home; she didn't want to talk to me or anyone else. She started being so quiet and distant toward me that I just chalked it up to the fact that I was married and she wasn't.

Then I noticed my dad treating one of my younger sisters the same way he had treated me: the icky sweet smile, the touch, and the look. I felt sick, very sick; I wanted to believe that I was just seeing things. I had always wondered if he was still having sex with my older sister Sherri, but I really wanted to believe that he wasn't. Sherri had moved back home after her divorce but I just kept telling myself no way.

Between the death of my baby Amanda, the birth of my sons, living away from home for a while and my continued sicknesses, I had missed the truth of what was really happening right before my eyes.

My sister Sherri had met a man and married him very quickly. This man, who had his own religious connections and did not agree with our family, said to me one day, "Your family worships your dad." I tried to argue, but deep inside I knew that something was very wrong. I couldn't form a whole sentence without saying, "my dad says." I claimed I agreed with every word he said, even if I didn't. I felt powerless. My brother-in-law showed me Matthew 24:4, "Jesus answered, watch out that no one deceives you. For many will come in my name, claiming, I am the Christ and will deceive many."

It was next to impossible at first for my mind to receive that message. Could my dad be teaching of Christ and still be deceiving the rest of the family and me? It was just the beginning, but God used my brother-in-law to help me understand that maybe not all that I was seeing was as it seemed.

Robert turned one in March of 1988, and there was real turmoil in my heart. I couldn't ignore all the signs I had started to see. My brother-in-law suspected that the baby my sister had had "early" was not actually his. My sister had become pregnant very soon after they had met, and after learning that there was sexual abuse in the family, he had started to wonder.

Then I noticed my brother, Sam, was very upset. He told me that my dad had slept with his wife. As I started to hear more and more, I realized this was a very sick situation. I finally went to my dad and said, "You promised that it would never happen again." His reply was that it was none of my business. I felt crushed and sickened. I knew that every suspicion I had about my younger and older sisters was true.

I discovered the truth when I started asking different family members who knew the truth. I felt I was losing my mind: I cried, I felt trapped; my plant nursery was on that property, my mobile home and all that I owned was on my parent's property.

It was February 1988, and Chris and I had finally saved enough money to build an addition to our mobile home, something that only a couple months before would have been so exciting for me. I had nothing, so it was a great thing to have more room.

I looked out the window one morning, and saw Chris and my dad starting to build. As I watched, a very strong emotion came over me, and an inner voice said as clear as can be, "if you don't leave this place, you will die."

At first, I just stood there watching, with all the feelings flooding through me: anger, confusion, and fear, fear, fear. How could I tell my dad I wanted to leave? Every attempt before had always lead to him telling us that it was not God's will, that we couldn't make it on our own. What do I do, oh my God, what do I do? With as much courage as I could muster, I walked out that door and said, "Stop, you need to stop." Both Chris and my dad looked at me with the strangest faces, and I said, "I'm not sure what I want, so please stop building." I said I needed to think.

A couple of days later I went and told my dad that I needed to go away and think. Somehow, I got a ticket to Texas to see my oldest sister on my dad's side, Jackie. I had never been on a jet plane and I was scared, but I didn't really care, I was twenty-two years old and I knew that the way I felt inside was absolutely more than I could deal with. I fought against losing complete control; I was so angry.

I left the kids with Chris, thinking they were safe with him with the help of my sister-in-law, but instead of him giving me room, he got on the next flight out to Texas and showed up at my sister's. When I had left, I had really been angry with him for many reasons, but when he arrived, he told me he would do anything to help me leave my parent's place. We would start over. We would make it. Life would be good, he promised. I believed him; I needed to.

We knew we would lose the plant nursery and our very livelihood that we had worked so hard for, at a time when profits were finally within reach. We could see a future in the business, to a degree; however, it was not worth it, as I realized how very sick my family was, particularly my dad.

Chris and I spent the week talking to each other and to my older sister, Jackie, about all the sickness, fear, pain, and confusion. After talking, Chris and I felt we were strong enough to go back and tell my dad we were leaving.

The very thought of telling my dad that we were leaving caused paralyzing fear, a fear I really can't put into words. It controlled my whole body, mind, and soul. I prayed, asking God to help me, please. I knew I had to leave; there was no other way. I knew for sure then, and when I look back, I know for sure now, that my Lord and Savior was with me every step of the way.

We arrived back home and the feeling on the property was very strange. Everyone looked at me very strangely; I couldn't really read them, but there was a definite avoidance everywhere we went.

I'm not sure of the exact words I said to my dad, but part of the conversation was that he promised he would not "touch" any of his daughters again and I had believed him, then I told him we were moving. I do remember his expression and his words as he told me I was not ready to leave; the same thing I had been told every time I had tried.

I tried a couple of other times to reason with my dad as we worked to get things done before leaving. I struggled with the emotions and plain fear of making such a move. I felt very strongly one moment that I was doing the right thing, and then the next, complete fear. I even tried to avoid the "real" reason we were leaving when I talked to my dad, telling him during one talk, "You see that orange you are eating, Dad? It's your orange and this is your property. I just want to discover what God has for me."

It was true that I wanted to see what else was out there, but the real reason was the sickness—pure sickness from every angle. I felt I needed to be honest with my dad and tell him what the real issue was, and when I finally told him that I felt he had a sexual demon, well, it wasn't taken very well, to say the least. He became so angry and he let me know that God would get me for saying that to him. I felt fear in a sickening way, but I knew that there was no turning back. I prayed and prayed, and just kept working to leave.

Chris spoke to a friend of his, and before we knew it, he had a job in Kingman, Arizona. I'm not sure how it all came about, but I know the hand of God was with us. We went to Kingman and were shown property that we could get for less than five hundred dollars an acre. No water, no electricity, nothing; just ranch land, forty-three acres for $19,500. We were so excited—a place of our own. I really didn't care that there were no amenities; I would be free, free free!

The day we left was very stressful and fearful and a touch exciting, but the fear made it hard even to think happy thoughts. Chris and I walked into the house and to the living room. My dad was sitting in his chair with the same face I had seen so many times: a face that brought fear because you just couldn't figure it out.

Chris and I said, "Well, we are leaving now; just wanted to let you know." My dad looked at us and said, "Well, I've thought about this a lot and I realize that it is a good thing that you are leaving, as God has some real hard knocks for you kids. God needs to set you straight."

One part of me was frozen; another was angry and just ready to get out. It was all I could take: it was already hard enough; I was already scared enough—and now he was pronouncing judgment on us? We said goodbye and left. There were no hugs, no God be with you, no we love you, can't wait to see you—just pain, fear, sadness, and a growing feeling that God didn't love me and that He was going to bring down judgment on me.

We made it to Kingman and to our new property and lived in our travel trailer while we waited for our ten-by-fifty mobile home to arrive. My days were busy at first, and even though I felt fear, I was able to push it aside for the first few days, as we had so much to do. Our three sons had to be cared for, and Chris had already started his new job, so each day was spent doing as much as I could to care for the boys in this little fifteen-foot trailer with no electricity and water only in jugs. It was crazy, but there was a very happy spot in my heart. After all, I had a husband who promised me we would be okay.

The mobile home finally was made level and we moved in. It had only taken about three weeks, but with three small boys, that was a long time. I buried myself with fixing up the trailer and putting everything back together after the move. I should have been happier and happier, but instead my dad's words rang in my ears night and day.

As soon as life had a little normal rhythm to it, I became horribly fearful, so fearful I could hardly breathe. I feared even to move, at times, literally fearing that if I got off the bed I would die. I cried; I panicked; I prayed. I tried to care for my sons, and I did, but many days I just went through the motions. I loved those boys so much; they were my life, my very reason for leaving Skull Valley. I knew it was so very sick there, yet I fought every day with the fear that I would die for leaving.

Then one day I woke up feeling very tired and in pain. All my lymph nodes were swollen behind my ears and down my neck. At the base of my skull, there was also painful swelling. I knew then that I was going to die. I just knew it. Gripped with paralyzing fear, I went through the morning caring for my boys but I just knew I was going to die. Then about three days later, the boys, also seeming very tired, said they hurt behind their ears, and when I looked, they had the same problem. God, how could you do this, are you going to let us all die? Please help me; I am so scared.

Was it right to leave Skull Valley? Was it right to tell my dad he had a sexual demon in him? Was God going to get me for it? Where do I hide? You can't hide from God. Oh, the panic was more than I could handle! But the sin—the sexual sin my dad kept committing—was it really sin? He said it wasn't. Who was I to question this man, who had been the one to know God and His word in a way that only he could. No one else in the world was as versed in the Bible as my dad; he was the one. It was his interpretation that was right; could anyone question that? I wrestled with these thoughts until exhausted; fear, horrible fear.

Then one day, I picked up the Bible I had been given at age sixteen; it had my name on the cover. I felt a little sick as I picked it up; it scared me to even really look at it. I had tried to read the Bible, but none of it had made much sense. So I thought I'd just start reading in Matthew. I did and then as I came to Matthew 11:28–30, I knew that God was talking to me.

Yes, this young lady, who had been so fearful that she had gone up against her dad and family, said, "This life you are living is wrong!" God spoke to me through His Word, and to this day, as I read, "Come to Me, all *you* who labor and are heavy laden, and I will give you rest. Take My yoke upon you and learn from Me, for I am gentle and lowly in heart, and you will find rest for your souls. For My yoke *is* easy and My burden is light." (Matt. 11:28–30, NKJV), I can still feel the release of pain, fear and burden being lifted from me. The tears came and afterward I could sleep.

The lumps behind our ears and down our neck took months to go away, but I realized that we probably were going to live. However, the tired feeling actually stayed for years and the swollen lymph nodes returned many times to all of us. When I finally had a doctor look at them when they returned, almost two years later, he had no idea what they might be, other than an allergy. But the lesson was clear: God was not going to just let me or my sons die.

I wish I could say that after my heavenly Father blessed me with Matthew 11:28–30, all was fine and good, and I lived happily ever after, but that is not how life or the healing process works. One day was okay, the next, filled with fear. I would start to enjoy a free feeling, but then a cloud would come over me. I went through a period when I couldn't even get out of the car after my husband drove me to the store because I was sure that if I got out, I would die, so I would just say, no, take me back home. It was crazy, but the fear was very real.

I would have several good days in a row and then I would hear something from my family and all the fear would return. One day, I looked out my window and suddenly I saw a yellow Volkswagen coming down my driveway. There was only one yellow VW that looked like that, and the sight of it froze my heart. I could hardly move; my heart raced, the blood drained from my head, and I said to Chris, "My dad's here." I couldn't believe it.

My dad, with his stoic face, came through the door of my home and I tried my best to welcome him. There wasn't much chitchat, as there never was with my dad; the visit was really about his needs so we got right to the point. He wanted to know why I was so angry with him. I assume word had gotten back from other family members that I was very upset about many things.

I don't remember everything that was said that day, but I did ask why he had treated me so badly as a child. Why was I beaten so much and called so many names? I'm not even sure of everything I asked. I do remember that the look on my dad's face didn't change very much as he said to me that he wasn't really sure why, but yes, he had probably treated me worse than any of the other children.

After he and my stepmother left, I fell completely apart. The fear and rehashing of all of it in my mind started again. The process of trying to remember why I had left, what I was doing, assuring myself that it wasn't wrong, and that I wasn't going straight to hell, was a very long one and would take days. I cried out to God, still so very afraid of Him.

A part of me knew beyond everything that I was doing what was right. In the beginning, that part of me was very, very small, but after going over the whole, hellish, sickening life of my family and the little Scripture I knew, I would finally find peace for a short time and start trying to put my life back together.

Time and time again, I went through this process of fearing, rehashing, and seeking, and each time I came out the other side with a little more peace and a stronger sense of right and wrong. The part of me that knew that what I was doing was right, continued to grow, but very slowly sometimes; so slowly that I became discouraged.

The first Christmas after leaving Skull Valley came, and with it came a wonderful gift of electricity. We had lived with a generator for nine months, and to have Christmas lights that year was wonderful.

I wanted to be "normal," whatever that meant, and worked very hard to be so. I had no idea how to be around people. I had learned how to sell plants and interact with them but I had no ideas or opinions of my own. Before I left Skull Valley, if I spoke to someone, I couldn't give my own opinion; I always said, "My dad says," and would give his opinion. I became aware of this issue during a conversation with a woman who bought plants from me. I must have said "my dad says" too many times, because she looked at me long and hard, with kind of a quizzical and sympathetic look, and said, "You must think an awful lot of your dad," then looked away. I quickly replied, "Oh yes, he is so wonderful." For some reason, that interaction was brought to mind several years later, and I was able to recognize my problem.

The recession was very hard, and jobs were nearly impossible to get. Chris had been laid off from his job but had heard that mines in Nevada were hiring, so he had set out to get a job. He had found one in Carver, Nevada. He had taken our little camp trailer to live in and the weather was brutal. I waited for him to find a place for us to live and we moved to a small place called Gillman Springs.

As soon as I saw the place, I realized I had pointed it out a couple of years earlier, while going to Oregon to get trees for our plant nursery, as a place I would never live! Well, God has a sense of humor and that was my first lesson in never saying *never*. We not only rented a mobile home there but also rented from the very man who owned all the old junk cars and old junk mining equipment, Wow, I really had to look at that and say, okay; maybe God is trying to show me something.

We moved in February of 1989. It was cold, the wind blew, and I was very lonely. I only spoke to family occasionally, and not many good things came from those talks—usually only more fear or sadness.

My health seemed to be getting better, though, and I was thankful. I had been on so many antibiotics for my tonsils that my immune system was very weak.

In November of 1988, I had come to a point of not being able to continue the way I was anymore. Facing a fear that I would die, I put aside a comment my dad had made about running from a bear only to meet a lion (meaning that, if I had my tonsils removed to fix the problem, I would only run into a bigger problem), and I had had them taken out.

It was the only time I had been in a hospital except when I had almost died from my tonsil infection, and yes, I was afraid. Yet, God gave me a peace when I surrendered to Him and said, I'm in Your hands. The surgery was tough and the healing slow, much slower than it should have been, but it was a very good thing. It was another situation where I could see that God was there for me. We made it through the winter in that little town so far from society, yet I tried to look at the positive. I found a little church to go to and started to meet a few people. I still had a fear of church though.

Chapter 13
The Phone Call

IT WAS A WARM SPRING MORNING, and I really had nothing of importance on my mind. We had moved into a mobile just down the way from the first place we had rented, but this one had an acre of land with it and was a rent-to-own. I was also much closer to a woman who really seemed to care about me.

She checked on me almost every day and was very good to the boys and me. She was very different in the sense that she was very forward, laughed a lot, and told me that she really cared about me. That was very uncomfortable for me, and I really had a hard time with it. As a child, no one had really expressed that they cared about me after I left my sister in Oklahoma. But as an adult, three people had told me they did, and had showed me affection: a couple I had met in Prescott, and now, Suzann, who would later become my adoptive mother. I was very uncomfortable with affection or love; that just didn't happen to me.

Then one morning the phone rang; I had no thought about who it might be and just answered it. The voice on the other end was one I didn't know at all. and at first it was hard to understand what he was saying. I do remember, "Hi, Mrs. Hansen, this is detective Smith with the Prescott Sheriff's Department," and then I blanked out for a while; I just remember feeling as though my heart had stopped as fear gripped me. I knew this was about my dad, and then it all came washing over me again. I just wanted everything to go away; all my pain, fear, uncertainty, and sadness, just to go away; to wake up with my whole world happy! "Mrs. Hansen, may I call you Paula?" Oh yes, I was on the phone! Yes, yes, you can call me Paula. "Paula, may I ask you a few questions about your family, or do you want to talk? We understand this may be very hard for you, but we really would like to know if there's anything you can tell us about your dad, Mr. Sanders, that could help us with our investigation."

It was a time of decision, but it took me only a few moments to answer. I knew I wanted my father stopped. I didn't want revenge, I wanted him stopped to save my younger sisters, whom I loved: Sisters whom I'd helped raise for many years, even sisters that might not even be born yet as he was still having children at that time. I also wanted to give my younger brothers a chance to be in a healthier situation.

Maybe they could grow up healthier than my older brothers, who had already hurt so many children, starting with me. I wanted the pain stopped in this family, and at that moment, I knew I would do whatever it took!

I can't tell you how many times over the next many years I wished I could just run away and believe that I was not even a part of all of this. Time and time again I knew I had to continue on this road because there were children that needed it done, even if they thought I was wrong, and believe me, all my younger siblings were taught that I was Satan, a demon in the flesh. They hated me and were very afraid of me for many years. Some came to think I had never been used by God, but only by Satan. I hurt so much; I felt so alone. I had only one sister who stood with me, my sister Ellie.

After talking to me for about thirty minutes, Detective Smith asked if it would be okay if he flew up to Nevada and came to my home to talk to me more. I agreed and wanted him to come. I went through a whole range of fear once again as I tried to deal with the confusion I felt about my family.

A sad feeling started to occur in me more and more as I tried to deal with the pain and fear I felt. My desires for God and to know Jesus better were numbed. I had a husband who had promised me that we would learn who God really is together, but instead, he had started lying to me, had gone back to smoking, had started going to the dance clubs and had really pulled away from me. I was horrified! How could this be? I was trying to deal with my dad, three small boys, all my emotions, and so much loneliness. I was trying to be normal in a world in which I had no idea how to live. I became very frustrated and angry. I started living in a world of make believe. If I didn't think about God, then he wasn't really there. I tried to convince myself daily that it was easier to just ignore my feelings than to deal with them, and I really wasn't sure if God loved me anyway.

After the detectives came (there were two of them, Detective Smith, and another whose name I could never remember), I recall how horribly uncomfortable it was talking about the abuse. To tell a complete stranger, and realize that what really had been done to me was not just in my mind, was horrible. I was reassured that everything was going to be taken care of, not to worry.

That is what caused all my worry day in and day out. I thought about the whole situation from beginning to end. I had to; it was the only way to get a little peace. I would start out full of fear, so full of fear I couldn't even move, rehashing from the time I was a little girl to present. As I looked at all of it, I could see clearly that what I was doing was the right thing to do. I had no other choice and I knew it. Finally, I would find a little rest inside. In my mind, this would be over in a matter of months After I met with the detectives, they would get an order; from there they would drive to Skull Valley, knock on the door, and arrest my father. We would have a trial and then life would start.

I could not have been more wrong in my assumption. Weeks passed, then months; a grand jury had indicted my dad but there was one small problem: even after many, many attempts to find my dad on his property in Skull Valley, they had had no success. Many rumors went through the "family," and I became very aware that much of the information was purposefully "sent out," such as that Dad is living in Alaska, or that one of my brothers is hiding him.

My emotions were on a roller coaster. Every time a small amount of normalcy came into my life, some kind of news from my family would come. It was exhausting.

I tried to go on living, but my marriage was starting to show some real problems. I tried to believe that everything was going to be okay. I would just fight to make it work; I would not believe in any way that Chris and I could ever have problems that would lead to divorce.

By April of 1989, just one year after leaving Skull Valley, lies had torn my marriage apart, but I hoped we would be okay.

Somewhere in the midst of it all, the decision was made to try for a little girl. By July, I knew I was pregnant, very pregnant: I had a tummy overnight. It was very strange, although at the time, I thought nothing of it, really, but then I started bleeding and had a lot of pain. The closest hospital was one hundred miles away.

I was scared, so I called Suzann and she came right over to watch the boys. Chris put me in the truck and drove me the one hundred miles. I just knew it was all over and I felt sad. I was in so much pain, and I just knew this was because God was mad at me. I was such a bad person; God wasn't going to bless me at all.

We reached the hospital, and after a pregnancy test and an exam, I was told it appeared that the baby was still intact and I would just have to be watched closely. I went home late that same day; the bleeding had nearly stopped and the cramping was almost gone.

I felt relieved and a little ashamed. I felt God didn't love me and that he didn't want to care for me, mostly because by this time I was really trying not to think of Him. I returned to the hospital one more time to see my doctor and was reassured that I was still pregnant.

In September, Chris was told that the mine he worked at to be closed down due to violations. I was shocked. I had finally started to build a relationship with Suzann and I really didn't want to leave, but we had no choice. Chris called his old boss in Arizona, and on a verbal promise of a five-year job opportunity, we headed back.

This pregnancy was different: I felt so much larger than the previous times. I knew I needed a doctor and started looking immediately, but I ran into problems. It would be weeks before I could see one, and because I was four months pregnant and had had another doctor before, I would have to come up with a large amount of money to get started. So I headed back to my midwife and started seeing her.

The first time I saw her, at four months, I was tired and kept spotting when I picked up anything too heavy. I had never had that problem with my other pregnancies. I was scared and tried to lie down whenever possible. I started having headaches during my fourth to fifth months. I just knew God was punishing me. I didn't dare let myself get to close too prayer because it was still more comfortable not to think about God.

When I arrived at my appointment, it was obvious that there was something different. Even my midwife knew there was, I had grown too fast. So blood work and an ultrasound were ordered. The blood work said that I was very anemic and so I started a good iron supplement and waited for the ultrasound.

I had to wait two weeks, and that was a very long time. I was very concerned that there was a real problem with my baby, and I felt very scared. I couldn't sleep and once again I just knew that God was going to punish me. I would lay on the couch for hours through the night, just hoping that everything would be okay. The only thing that gave me peace was that there was so much movement. I was so big that I kept thinking that there had to be two babies in there!—and then I would fall asleep. But the next day it all started again.

We received the papers in the mail for COBRA insurance but decided that we just couldn't afford the three hundred and fifty dollars to keep it, so we canceled it. What a huge mistake! We would pay for that many times over.

The day finally came to go for the ultrasound, and I was both excited and scared. I dressed the three boys and, with a friend, headed to my appointment.

It only took a few seconds to see that there was more than one baby, and I was so elated, I can't even tell you! I laughed and laughed. I felt so blessed, so very blessed. I couldn't quit smiling; I smiled for days—no birth defect, as I had feared—just two very healthy, twenty-three-week babies. My hope that I was carrying girls faded quickly as I learned by looking at the ultrasound results that I was carrying two boys. After a very short period of disappointment, I just felt blessed. I told Chris, and he was shocked.

One day the phone rang and it was my sister Ellie. She said that the family was saying that I was having twins because I had taken birth control, and now God was punishing me with twins. You're only blessed when you have one at a time. I was so crushed: for one, I had never taken birth control, and for another, could this mean I was cursed? I was heartbroken. I cried as another joy seemed to be stolen from me. The words of my family still had so much power. Why, why, why!? I tried to forget their comments and keep enjoying the pregnancy.

I was very large and became more miserable every day. Caring for the other three boys became very difficult, but doing so did make me happy. I had to see a doctor now, since a midwife is not allowed to deliver twins; it is just too risky. I was fine with that and scheduled an appointment with the only doctor that would both accept me at this late stage and work with my midwife. The only problem: he lived three and one-half hours from my home. I had to make the drive myself, with only the boys, most times. I had to see the doctor every two weeks because twins were high risk.

We realized it would be impossible to put two more children in the ten-by-fifty mobile and worked very hard to get a larger place. We found a sixteen-by-eighty, three- bedroom, two-bath with a fireplace and wonderful kitchen. I was ecstatic. I had never lived in such a wonderful place; I felt like a princess. It was only about five years old. I felt rich. We moved in the week before Christmas, and had a wonderful Christmas.

On December 29, I started vomiting at about 2:00 in the afternoon. I called Chris and told him I was very sick and was starting to worry, as I felt labor pains. They occurred only about every five minutes, but still, they worried me.

Then I called my midwife and talked to her. She said I should worry only if they got closer together. It was very cold and was beginning to snow, something quite unusual for Kingman. By that time, Chris had come home from work, and I realized the contractions were much closer together, more like every two or three minutes. I was scared and called the midwife again. She told me I should head to the hospital in Kingman to be checked out.

Our neighbor was a sweet woman, not in the best health but she came right down and sat with the boys. I was thankful, but was so sick and weak I hardly remember even talking to her. We left and headed to Kingman, sixteen miles away. When we arrived at the hospital, I hoped that they would take care of me. The contractions were two minutes apart. I was starting to have the all-too-common feeling that God was mad at me and was going to let me and my babies die.

Because I didn't have insurance, the only two ob–gyn doctors in town refused to see me. The emergency doctors weren't quite sure what to do with me, so they just wheeled me to a room and left me there. The hospital wanted to discharge me and have me drive to another hospital; however, there was no other hospital for at least ninety miles: in Las Vegas, Nevada. There were about four inches of snow on the ground by then. About that time, a nurse from St. Joseph's hospital in Phoenix, who was working at the Kingman hospital that night, told me she would get me help even if she lost her job. I later found out she did lose her job; I will be forever grateful for her kindness and I'm sure that God made it up to her.

Even though I didn't realize it then, my God would provide for me time and time again, just as He did on this occasion. After many phone calls to my doctor in Cottonwood—the only one who would see me without insurance—I was told that medication would be started to stop the contractions and I would be airlifted to St. Joseph's in Phoenix. I was terrified: why couldn't the doctors here just see me? I didn't understand.

The ambulance arrived, and the medication was started that helped to stop the labor, but it made me very ill. I was soon on an airplane—not a chopper as I had feared so much, but a plane. I knew a plane could go down, too, in bad weather, but a plane just seemed better.

When we arrived in Phoenix, the wind was blowing. I remember that the sheet kept blowing up as I was being carried; I was miserable, embarrassed, sick, and scared. I stayed in the hospital three days, and on New Year's Eve, 1990, I was released, but asked to stay in Phoenix so that I would be close if there were problems.

The following day, I was told I could go home. I went to see my regular doctor a few days later. He asked me to move closer, since I was almost two hundred miles away and he was not comfortable with that, so I moved in with my newly married sister, Ellie, who lived much closer, and waited. I was still on medication to stop the contractions; I was quite miserable, and sleep was almost impossible.

The babies were due on March sixth, and it was only the beginning of January. Every day seemed a year. It was hard on my sister to have us there. I grew very fast, and saw the doctor every week. At end of January, I quit the medication, since I wasn't having any more contractions. Then came February, and when I went to the doctor on Friday, February 16, I was told I needed to go to the hospital: the babies were going to be born.

Matthew was born first, just as we had thought; we had already named them when they could no longer move from side to side. After some difficulty, David was born breach, but both were healthy. I was overjoyed: they were beautiful, and I felt blessed.

I was released from the hospital the next day, but the babies couldn't go; it's a law that twins have to stay a day longer. I was in so much pain I couldn't even walk, and leaving my babies nearly killed me, but without insurance, I had to leave. I slept very little; I worried about Matthew and David at the hospital and my three older boys with Chris's parents, with whom they had never stayed alone.

After being released from the hospital with the babies, we drove to Prescott, where our other boys were. It was beginning to snow, so I was thankful when we arrived safely. William, Aaron, and Robert were so excited. Two babies: Can we look? Can we touch? Can we hold them?

But the fun and joy were quickly over when my father-in-law started cursing at the older boys and telling them that they were not to touch the babies. Don't even touch them, "you will put a hole in their heads."

Robert, who was not quite three, was deeply hurt. All three boys felt hurt because they had been promised they would be able to see me at the hospital as soon as the babies were born; my father-in-law had said yes at first, and then no. That was very common for him, but the boys were too young to comprehend. Something happened in Robert that night and it would take him years to like those babies. He was angry and tried pinching, hitting, or taking things away from them for many years.

We left the next day, even though there were fourteen inches of snow on the ground. I was not going to stay even one more day. We drove very carefully home. I hadn't been home for seven weeks and I was so excited. I still hadn't moved in completely when I had had to leave, and there was so much to do, but the doctor had ordered that I was not to do anything more than necessary. It had been very difficult to stop the bleeding and the possibility of more problems was there.

The next morning was Monday, and Chris took William to school. I was to pick him up at 10:00 a.m. I was dizzy, weak, and still in pain, but I readied the twins—now four days old— Aaron, three, and Robert, almost three years old. It was already 9:30 and it would take thirty minutes to go the sixteen miles to town; four of those miles on very rough dirt roads. I got all the boys in the car, sat down to start the car, and realized it was not going to start. The battery was dead; it had been giving us problems, but Chris had said it would be fine. What would I do now? William had to be picked up, and we had no phone so I couldn't call the school: I couldn't even call for help.

The nearest neighbor was two miles away. The February wind was blowing hard and it was still very cold. But I had no choice; my son would be so scared. I was never late to pick him up and he was only five. I panicked; I put the twins in a stroller, covered them well, put coats on Aaron and Robert, had them hold on to the stroller, and we started walking.

As I walked, I knew that I was in going to be trouble if I started bleeding again, but I had no choice. I still had about a half-mile to go when I saw a truck coming. It was one of my husband's friends, Ray. He pulled up beside me and, before I could say a word, yelled, "Hey, it's good to see a woman out walking off the baby fat." I was so angry and close to tears that I ignored him and continued walking. I arrived at my neighbor Betsy's house, and asked her husband to help me. He drove us back to our house and jumped my car. I was so thankful: tired, but thankful.

I drove to town as fast as possible, and when I arrived at the school, William was very distraught but glad to see me. I headed straight to Sears. I told the man at the counter that I needed a battery. I explained that I needed to sit down. I truly was delirious by now and the man was very concerned. After I paid, he quickly agreed to change the battery, even though it was something they normally did not do. After it was all done, I drove home.

That night, when Chris arrived home, I told him what had happened. He just looked at me and asked how I had paid for it. I told him, with a credit card, and he said you shouldn't have done that. Anger came up in me that I couldn't explain; it made me hurt so bad that he would not even show any concern. This type of behavior on his part became the norm for us: he became more detached and I became angrier.

By the time the twins were six weeks old, I couldn't keep up with them on the milk supply. I nursed them, but they were still hungry, so when my goat gave birth to triplets, I milked her morning and evening. The twins thrived. I loved my new home and I tried to be happy every day, but the phone started to ring with calls from collectors.

When the twins were three weeks old, Chris lost his job with the mining company that had promised five years of work. This made us ineligible for any state help; we would have to pay for everything from preterm labor problems to the births. The figures were overwhelming, and I had no idea what to do. I cried a lot and tension rose between us.

Chris did as little as possible to help me with the children, even pushing them away as he came through the door after work. I would spend time getting them excited to see him, only to have him come in too tired to show even affection, let alone spend true time with them. I wanted more for my children; I wanted them to experience love. I tried every day to give them what I never had, and I wanted Chris to do the same. The sadness and fear mounted as I realized I was hoping for something that probably would never happen, but still I tried.

We were still hauling water, and with two newborns and three very active boys, the water went fast. I asked Chris to bring home water nightly, but it seemed to be too much trouble, so his answer to the problem was to say: use less water. It was so hard, because I needed to have things clean. I had grown up in filth and it was more than I could deal with as an adult.

Chris started working for a water drilling company and met a man who wanted to be friends with him. I hadn't met him yet, but Chris told me that he seemed all right. After I met him, I really didn't think much, but I guess for Chris it was different.

This man had a way of hauling one thousand gallons of water at a time and offered to bring it to us. Chris agreed, and at first when he brought the water, I just stayed inside. One day I went out to say hi and thank him for the kind gesture. He asked Chris to call him, as he wanted just to hang out with him. I thought it was a good idea since the few men Chris talked to were not so great. But Chris, for whatever reason, had begun to avoid this man and I felt sorry for him and somewhat guilty; after all, he brings us water and wants to be friends with Chris, who ignores him. So, I took it upon myself to just be kind to him. It was a mistake; I would end up committing adultery with this man and putting myself in a very bad place before it was all over.

I started the relationship when the twins were only about four months old and found out I was pregnant a short time later. I lived for many years with the pain of not knowing who the father of my baby girl was. Later, we had a DNA test done, which showed Chris was her father.

I very shortly admitted to the affair and tried to break away from the relationship but at first just couldn't. Finally, swallowed up in guilt, I left the affair and tried to work it out with Chris. I begged him to get counseling with me to find out why he had some of the problems he had and so I could work on mine. I begged him, and he finally agreed. I asked for one more thing: since he had moved out and was already living elsewhere, could he please just stay in that place while we put our marriage back together. It was at that time that he pulled out a yearbook and asked me, "Can you see this picture?" It was quite dark in the vehicle we were in, so he turned on the light and pointed to the picture of a young girl. He said, "If I can't move back in tonight, then this is who I'm going to date." Of course, I was so angry that I got out of his vehicle, went back to my car, and went home.

The anger continued and I packed up and moved to Cottonwood to be closer to my doctor and farther away from Chris and the affair.

I was so sick with the pregnancy that I could hardly function. I was sick at heart as well. I had ruined my marriage and I blamed myself completely. I still had feelings for the man I had the affair with, but I wanted to make my marriage work. I called Chris and we talked. We decided that we would try again, and I moved back to Kingman. My hopes were high that Chris and I could make it. He told his girlfriend that he wanted to try to save his marriage, so again we tried. Chris agreed that it didn't matter whose baby I was carrying, he just wanted to have our marriage back.

The first night back home, I was nervous, tired, and hungry. Foods were still an issue and only a few stayed down; potatoes were one of them, but the house was empty of any potato choices. I asked Chris to go the four miles to the truck stop and please get me a potato. His reply was, "There's peanut butter in the cupboard, eat that." I explained to him I couldn't eat the peanut butter, it would make me sick, but he just ignored me. The anger returned immediately and I realized I had made a mistake. This man was still the same selfish, uncaring man he had always been. Sex and owning me were the only important things to him.

Just a few days before Christmas it had gotten very cold; snow and freezing temperatures along with winds made it so we had to heat the water pump so we could have running water in the morning.

We had a fireplace and had put wood in it before going to bed that night. I had closed the glass doors and had checked everything, as I always did. The tree lights were off, the fire was safe, the boys were all sleeping, and well, the house was peaceful.

I still had the feeling daily that there was dishonesty between Chris and me: I had told him all of my wrongs, but I still felt that Chris was lying to me about one of my questions. I needed an answer, I needed him to be truthful; but for now, I just wanted Christmas to be wonderful. I crawled into bed. Chris was already fast asleep.

It was the time of year I thought about Amanda, since she had been born on December 19 and had died on the twenty-fourth. I laid there only for a brief moment, remembering her and the fact that she would have been nine years old. What would she have been like? I guess I would wonder forever. I drifted off to sleep.

Suddenly I was awake, coming very awake. I woke to a very strange feeling; I thought, "Why I'm I awake"? I lay there for a brief moment, and then I smelled smoke—bitter smoke. My mind raced. I knew it was not a normal smoke. I got out of bed, calling to Chris that I smelled smoke. I opened the door to our room and the smoke was very thick. I ran down the hall and saw flames through the window, but that couldn't be. It must be a reflection of the fireplace—it must be plugged—but when I looked at the fireplace, there was no flame. I realized then that really it was outside.

By then, Chris was standing there barefooted and in his shirt and underwear. We realized the fire was under the house. He ran outside. The light in the pump house had shorted out, causing a fire that had burned the pump house down, and then, because of the wind, the fire had gone under the house and started burning the insulation. Chris grabbed at the insulation, ripping it out with his bare hands and throwing it away from the house. It had gone about thirty feet along the underside of the home.

After Chris had put out the fire, I opened the house up to let the horrible toxic smoke out. It took at least an hour to get it all out, and it made me cough until I could hardly breathe. Even though we opened all the windows and it got very cold in the house, the boys never woke up through the whole thing. I checked on them, of course, and made sure they were okay, but it made me realize that if I had not been awakened that night, we certainly would have died; I truly believe that Jesus was there protecting us and that He had an angel wake me up that night.

Chris had reacted very quickly that night and had kept the house from burning down. The fire had started up into the washer and dryer hookups and in only a few more minutes, it would have been a much different story. Chris's hands had been burnt and his feet cut up from running on the rocks that night. It was one time that, as I watched him, I felt protected. It took some doing, but with the help of some good neighbors, we had a new pump house and water by Christmas.

Christmas came and went, and then Valentine's Day fast approached. I still felt that Chris was not being honest with me on an issue. Oh, he had always answered my question with the same, "No way, I never did that; don't worry, I would not have ever done that to you." I would say, "But Chris, are you sure? Just be honest, I need to know. Why do I feel you are not being truthful?" The answer was always the same. But I just had to ask again. It was Valentine's Day; he had brought me some chocolates and a card. I tried to be happy, but I still felt lied to and so I asked once again, Chris, I need to know, I feel you are not telling me the truth and maybe you are, but I feel you are lying. Please, did you sleep with my younger sister, did you, Chris? Please tell me if you did. He looked down, then looked at me and said, "Yes I did, but you cheated, too."

He was right, I had cheated, but this was different: it was my younger sister. I felt so filthy, so infiltrated by my family. How could he have done this? I couldn't breathe. Other women I could forgive and then get over, but even if I said I forgave this, I wasn't sure I could get over it. It just made me feel as if I were now part of the incest in my family, along with my husband. I had often felt that at least our marriage was not part of the filth of my family, and now it was. I tried very hard to push my feelings about this aside, but it nagged at me almost daily. I would pray, cry, and ask God to help me, and then I would try to continue living.

My baby was due in May, and I was looking forward to the birth. I was very tired, caring for five boys daily as well as performing all the other duties included with everyday life.

I often longed for a mother or sister to help me, not so much with the physical duties but just to be there. I longed for that, but the distrust I felt for most women was great. I only heard from Suzann occasionally; she had had a stroke and was very ill, and we lived so far apart at this time.

I did have one-woman friend, Gayanne Waller; she was kind, and I allowed her friendship. She was older than I, and her daughter would babysit at times. Gayanne and her family brought joy and love to me. Bob Waller would often tell me I was his fifth child. And Gayanne treated me as such.

Life was still not easy, and at times I really felt I couldn't handle any more. The pregnancy was rough and the marriage was in shambles; fear and the feeling of rejection were with me constantly.

Then the phone rang, and this time it was my sister Ellie. It seems she had decided to go down to Skull Valley unannounced; it was a rule that no one was to go to our home without calling first, that rule was not to be broken. The rule seemed strange, since according to various family members, my dad was not living on the property.

Even the sheriff's department had searched many times and had not found him. So why shouldn't we arrive unannounced? Well, leave it to Ellie to break the rule. She told me that she had arrived at the property needing really to use the bathroom, which was still an outhouse, after the drive from Prescott to Skull Valley

She walked up to the door and as she went to open it, it opened and out walked my dad. She said she nearly wet her pants. My dad, looking quite surprised said, "What are you doing here? You didn't call first." Then he said, "Well I'm glad you came to see me, because I've wanted to talk to you." It seems he wanted to have her go to the detectives and tell them that she had lied about what had happened to her. This he requested with a heap of guilt added, trying to prove his innocence through the Bible, as well as saying that, if she really loved him, she would do this.

He also stated that he understood that she could go to jail for a couple of years for having lied to the courts, but that it was the right thing for her to do. She was stunned; he then added that he wanted her to call me to ask if I would talk to him.

When she called me, I asked her what it was about, and she told me it was the same as what he was requesting of her. I felt so much fear I thought I would pass out. I told Ellie I would think about it. I hung up the phone and walked into the kitchen.

I had become so involved in the conversation that I hadn't noticed the twins with the only baby picture I had of myself. I was about four to six months old in the picture, and it was an eight-by-ten. The pieces lay on the floor and at first, I just felt really sad because it was the only picture of me that I had at that age. I started to cry. I cried for the picture, cried because of the phone call, and cried for all the confusion I felt. When I picked up the pieces, it was as if it were another picture, one of much more importance.

The picture had been torn at an angle across the chest area and across my head. A feeling of strength came to me as I looked at that picture. It was all clear, I knew then that I had to call the detectives and tell them that my dad had contacted me, that he was in Skull Valley, and that he wanted to talk to me, to try to get me to say I lied about the whole thing, even if it meant jail time for me.

The confusion was gone. I could see clearly that he had torn me apart. Both my mind and my heart had been torn, torn beyond repair. I knew I couldn't stand by and let him hurt me anymore, not if I could help it.

Shaking out of control, I picked up the phone and dialed the detective's number. I could hardly believe the words that came from my mouth as I told the detective everything. He encouraged me to call my dad back and tell him that I would meet with him, and he promised my dad would never arrive at my home; he would be apprehended before he ever reached my home.

It was almost more than I could think about, and my heart raced with fear; I hadn't even spoken to my dad in almost four years. Would I even be able to speak when I called him, let alone ask him to meet with me, knowing I had arranged for his arrest? After telling the detective that I would call my dad and then call him back, I hung up.

I went through so many emotions, fear and sadness. Then I realized that, yes, he had ripped up my head and torn my heart, just as the twins had done to my baby picture. But that was not enough to call the detective; after all, I was free from him … But then the picture became very clear: I had to stop him from hurting any more children. He had already sexually abused three of my younger sisters and I still had four more and many younger brothers who would see that behavior as acceptable. The decision was made in that moment and with courage, I called my dad.

He answered the phone and a small knot rose in my stomach, but I was able to say, "I understand you would like to talk to me," He replied, "Yes, I would like to come to your place." I agreed and said goodbye. I was shaking but felt a peace that what I was doing was the right thing. I called the detective back and told him that my dad was on his way.

He reassured me that my dad would not arrive at my home, but a big part of me was scared beyond words. I sat and waited, I waited for about two and one-half hours, knowing that it should not take that long for an arrest; he lived only twenty minutes out of Prescott, so I became quite nervous.

Finally, the phone rang and it was my older brother, Tom, who had hurt me so much as a child. The first words out of his mouth were, "How dare you put an old man in prison, you cold bitch," For a moment I was stunned, then the words came and I said, "He had to be stopped; he never would have stopped on his own. Can you try to remember the prison he put us all in when we were children?" I'm not sure who hung up on whom, I just remember standing there realizing that it didn't matter what this man did, he always seemed the most important.

A short time later the phone rang and the detective said that my dad was in custody; he said he was sorry it took so long to call back, but many things had to be done with my dad, and it had taken time. He had only made it five or so miles from his house in Skull Valley before he was arrested.

Later I found out from my stepmother that my dad had been in Skull Valley the whole time, hiding in tunnels he had made from the basement of the house to the shop that was a short distance from it. He also had a four-by-eight bunker under the shop in which he lived. He often had her go there at night to read to him.

They both nearly died one night when he had her bring a bucket of coals down into the bunker to help keep it warm; the carbon monoxide had nearly killed them. When she finally woke up the next day, it was already noon. The children had no idea where she was and the baby was still in the crib crying and of course had been the same diaper as the night before. They were very sick for quite a time from that.

Part of me was relieved; the other part asked, what now? I knew this meant a trial but when, and how long? It had already been four years. I was tired, my marriage was in shambles, and I was a mess. Praying was done somewhat as a plea; , but I was too afraid to believe,

I knew my life was not what it should be. Day after day I wrestled with who God was; my fear raged at times such as this.

I started to get a few more phone calls from the prosecuting attorney's office. There were so many questions: the same ones over and over. I knew they needed to make sure about this—there were too many young children not to make sure. Still, my marriage was a mess, and I was a wreck. And this only added to it.

My daughter, Marie, was born April 17, 1991. She wasn't due until the middle of May, but on April 16, I picked up a baby goat and lifted it over the fence. I thought I was fine until shortly afterward. I felt as though I had wet my pants; it turned out my water had broken and so the trip to the hospital two hundred miles away was imminent. I was scared, as I knew I was not due for almost another month.

We went to the doctor's office because he wanted to make sure it was my water, and after a quick exam I was sent to the hospital. It was a very long and miserable delivery that almost turned into a C-section, but God is good; my daughter was born just shortly after midnight on April 17.

I felt blessed, but then all the fears came back of my first daughter, and this little one was the smallest baby I had ever had. She was six pounds, five ounces at birth and quickly lost seven ounces. I was so worried. She had a very hard time nursing and I was very scared. I couldn't bear the thought of losing this one also. I prayed and cried, asking God to help me with her.

A few weeks after Marie was born, my very dear friends, Bob and Gayanne Waller, gave me a baby shower for her. It was the only baby shower I had ever had. I was so excited, I couldn't even think. It was all done so well, and I received so many wonderful things for her. In addition, there were big brother gifts for all the boys! Wow, such love and concern I had *never* known before. I didn't know what to say, it was such a great thing; and yet I felt I should not receive such nice things.

My daughter was only a few months old when a pretrial was held for my dad. I'm not sure what it was about but I still remember fear that so consumed me that I couldn't even think straight. I do remember seeing my husband holding my little girl in that courtroom and thinking to myself that my dad would get to see her that day and never again. I felt a great sadness and a very deep hurt as I realized how much his sin had hurt all of us.

He had cheated my siblings and me out of a dad and all of the grandchildren out of a grandpa! I saw a depth to the pain that day that was so clear that it has remained with me throughout the choices I have made in my life. It became so clear that selfish, sinful choices hurt so many, and mine was just a small portion of the pain this man caused. A lonely sadness came over me, as it would many times to come over the years. I have reflected on this truth many times and still do to this day.

As with every major situation with my family, it took me several weeks to pull myself back together. The emotions were more than I could deal with. I realized after my last baby was born that I should not be having any more babies. I had a tubal ligation done. I went through feelings of guilt since I had been taught that was a sin. However, I was truly so overwhelmed, I really didn't care. It was just too much to think about more children, and I had no way to raise them.

I decided about the time of the first trial that I needed to get my GED. I was so scared at the prospect of school that I almost didn't do it, but then I didn't see any other way.

I had to, so I signed up for a program under the JTPA (Job Training Partnership Act) and started attending class to get that GED. It was hard, and I had to put the three youngest in daycare while I went to school.

It was hard to focus on going to school for a GED with my marriage a mess, the thought of the coming trial, and while taking care of six very small children.

I had also started going out, getting drunk, and doing really stupid things. I felt so out of control and yet I felt less fear; I really just felt less! It was fun in a way and I justified my behavior by saying at least I'm not sexually abusing children, lying, and using God's name to control people.

When Marie was about nine months old, she came down with a fever and cough, and then breathing problems. I was so scared; I took her to our doctor and was told she needed a breathing treatment. I was very naive about that sort of thing and just wanted her to get help. I didn't realize that there was something more serious going on.

The next day she was worse, so I took her back to the doctor. I was informed that they were out of tubing for a treatment, so I would have to wait until the next day or go to the hospital.

I left his office and started driving south about a mile. I looked down and realized my daughter was turning blue. I panicked. I looked up and the hospital was right there, so I pulled in, my heart pounding and my mind racing. Not again, please God, I can't go through this again.

I ran through the emergency room doors and "said to the first person I saw, "Please help, my baby isn't breathing right." She was taken from me and I watched as the nurses tried to give a breathing treatment. It didn't work, so she was stripped down and I remember a shot being given, then oxygen, and then I heard her cry. I felt so relieved, so very scared and so alone—and yes, with the very familiar feeling and thought that God must hate me.

I spent the next four days in the hospital with my baby girl as she fought to get her air. She was tested for RSV but came back negative; however, I was told that she still probably had it. After four days, she could breathe on her own without oxygen as long as she had at least two breathing treatments a day.

That was my job also. It added so much stress and she was no help; if she couldn't breathe because something set off her asthma, she would just go somewhere, lie down and get very quiet. I would find her with blue lips and fighting to breathe. It was so hard to put her to bed at night. I loved it when she woke me up, but when she overslept I had to force myself to check on her. The question was always there: will she be okay?

I studied hard and became very determined to get my GED, realizing that I needed a job to help raise these children.

Chapter 14
The Trial

THE NOTICE CAME THAT THE TRIAL for my dad would be held at the end of July 1991. I was to take my GED test on my twenty-seventh birthday. How would I do all of this? I felt crazy with stress, fear, and sadness. How can I do it all? No help from my husband: he was just another weight around my neck.

I asked God to help me, half believing, half not. I was a mess, but even then, as I look back, there was a seed of faith beginning to grow even though I wasn't actually aware of it at the time.

The time grew nearer for the trial and my GED. It was hard to focus on my schooling. But determination grew in me as the trial came closer. I started saying small things such as, "I refuse to let my dad keep me in his grip any longer," or, "He owned me for the first twenty-two years of my life, but no more. I am free and I can live that way."

I prayed harder, still with very high levels of fear, guilt, and shame. How can I go through with the trial? I went through it so many times in my mind I thought I would go crazy, and always the answer came up the same: This was not about me; this was about my younger sisters. I wanted so badly to protect them. I wanted them never to feel the fear, shame, pain, and hopelessness I had felt, never, never, never!

Thinking of my younger siblings gave me daily strength, even though the messages kept coming through the grapevine that I was Satan and full of evil. The remarks hurt but I couldn't stop. I knew that the younger siblings had been brainwashed and I needed to protect and try to help them even more! I found great comfort in knowing that I might save even one of my sisters from the fate that I, and at least three younger and three older sisters, had lived through. I knew the pain and suffering we had endured and would for many, many years to come. To save even one was worth it.

After many calls and interviews, the trial was ready. We had to be early to trial so we were put up in a hotel in Prescott.

It was a time I was not proud of; I had started drinking more and that night my sister, our husbands and I went down on whiskey row and drank. I was so scared and actually felt fear at a level that I can't even put into words. Even though I knew I was doing the right things, part of me still felt that maybe, just maybe, God loved my dad more and so He would just let me die. It was a horrible place to be, and for the moment, drinking numbed that feeling.

We went back to the room but sleep wouldn't come. I dozed off a couple of times but mostly just tossed and turned. The reality was that the next day I would have to tell, in explicit detail and in front of complete strangers, what had happened to me as a child. Even worse, every family member who was old enough and wanted to, would be there in the courtroom.

My two older half sisters, Louise and Sue, would testify that day about my dad's abuse of them, even though he would not spend one day in prison because of what he did to them, there testimony was necessary to show a pattern of abuse .

At the time of this trial, there was a statute of limitations on sexual abuse. Since the time of their abuse, the law had changed in the state of Arizona, as well as many other states.

The only charges that would send my dad to prison that day were from my sister Ellie and me. A younger sister and an older sister refused to talk.

Most of the blame for the trial was placed on me; all the family was convinced that I was some sort of a ringleader who had talked my other sisters into this.

Well, I can say that the younger half sister that finally refused to testify was very fearful, and would agree to testify one day, and then change her mind the next; I tried to help her through her fears, because the only reason she hesitated to testify is that she was so afraid of losing the family's love. I could understand her, but even though I was scared, daily I was convinced more and more that what I was doing was what God wanted me to do.

Morning came and there I was, ready to go, realizing that that day would be the toughest day of my life. I needed God to help me, so I asked. I knew that the reflection of God in my life was very poor and that my life was lousy, but I still asked. I felt a calm and quiet strength; I knew that I was helping all my younger sisters and brothers on that day.

We walked to the courthouse from the hotel; it was a warm day and very beautiful. I can remember thinking, such a beautiful day and so much sadness.

We arrived at the courthouse, and security was high. There was concern that one of my family members might try to hurt someone. We made it through security and met up with the prosecutors one last time, going over all the issues as they tried to calm us.

I have a hard time remembering many details of the hearing; the quiet strength and calm I felt earlier turned to numb fear as I walked into the courtroom. The fear was strong but my inner strength was stronger. I knew I would make it through the day. As we walked in, I was very aware of many family members seated on my dad's side of the courtroom. Only a few were on our side. The tension was so thick and I realize, as I reflect now, why it was so hard to remember some of the details. The pressure was sickening, and I felt numb with sadness and fear.

I finally had the courage to really look around me, and when I did I saw my dad; he looked so small, feeble, and harmless. Could he really be the man who had caused so much fear and pain? He sat there with a strange look I can't even describe. He was so calm, as if to say, "I did nothing wrong, so why should I be sad or in fear? I'm innocent."

There was security everywhere. It was somewhat reassuring, yet quite scary, too. I knew the power my dad had over my brothers, and I knew that they would consider hurting people should they believe my dad wanted them to. I later found out that one of my brothers had actually left his home with a loaded gun, with full intentions of killing Ellie first and then going to my home and killing me, I'm not sure what the circumstances were that stopped him, but I'm sure it was because of God!

The jurors entered the room and as they sat down, I could think of nothing but that I would have to say many horrible things in front of these people;—but they had to be said.

"All rise," I heard the bailiff say, and my heart stopped. We all stood, and the proceedings started: first my sister Louise, then Sue. I looked at my dad: no expression change at all. But, to look at family members brought looks that said: how dare you lie about our dad; you're the bad one, we know it because he told us how bad you are.

I knew that my time was coming and that it truly was going to be the hardest thing I would ever do. The jury sat there with faces that you just couldn't read, yet I thought I saw pain in their eyes.

Oh no, was that my name? I got up, walked to the front, and was sworn in. I sat down and the questioning began. I answered all the questions. I know I did, but I couldn't tell you the answers. I know it was painful; I know I had to identify my dad, and when I did, his expression never changed. He just had a look that said, "I'm innocent."

When I was done, I remember my legs were so weak and wobbly it was hard to walk from the witness stand back to my seat. I was shaking and I hurt.

Next, it was my sister Ellie's turn, and I will forever remember her as she was questioned and while she answered. When she was done, she turned to my dad and through tears and so much pain she asked him, "Why, why did you do it? Why did you hurt us so badly? You ruined us, why?" She was crying so much it was hard to understand her.

The jury fought to stay composed, and yet my dad's expression stayed the same. It was very unreal and very sad. I cried; I hurt for my sister so much.

The trial was very short, only one day. My dad refused an attorney, stating he had done nothing wrong and that God would exonerate him one day.

My emotions were hard to understand that day, and to this day I know it was the hardest, scariest thing I ever did. After the state had put us all on the stand, my dad was questioned once again, still with no expression change and no remorse; just a look of disbelief. He answered no contest.

The jury was dismissed and so were we. I felt too sad, too scared, and too sick to my stomach even to try to figure out the jury's findings.

Finally, after what seemed like forever, we were told in the late afternoon that Friday that the jury was ready. My heart stopped; I felt weak and somewhat numb with fear. We filed into the courtroom, and looking at the jury, there were such sober looks on their faces it was hard to say what they were thinking at that time. However, after the reading of the jury findings, in which my dad was found guilty of thirteen counts of child sexual abuse, there were such feelings in that courtroom. Horror on my dad's side of the room, thankfulness on ours; yet there was still no change in my dad. As for the jury, I will never forget them.

The judge gave the order that my dad be held until sentencing, and he was taken away. Then the jury, tears running down many of their faces, stood and asked to hug each of us. It was such a strange feeling, I had never had hugs that were so warm and caring from complete strangers.

For a moment, I truly felt as if I weren't crazy, as my family always tried to say I was. My family acted as if what had happened to us was no one's business: it was a family thing and no one had the right to know about it. They said it was our fault; we caused it, and we wanted it. The hardest to overcome was the belief that it was God's will. But there in that courtroom, all the insanity was played out to sane people who helped me realize I wasn't crazy; my family was.

The next day was Saturday, August 2, my twenty-seventh birthday; but of more importance that was the day of the GED test I was going to take. I had studied long and hard to get my GED, and with the trial just one day behind me, I was an emotional mess. I was determined to take that test and pass it. Once again, scared, praying, and feeling as if I would fail, but too determined to give up, I mentally prepared for the test. I had to do this. I had to take the test and pass it. I knew my children needed me to help provide a better life for them. I wanted a better life for my children. It would take a few weeks to find out that I had passed, but when I did, oh what joy! I had done it! I smiled for days. It may have been a small thing to some, but for me it was the beginning of a new positive view of myself.

The sentencing was sometime in September, although I don't remember when; I just knew that I needed to be there, and I was, along with the rest of the family. It was a painful, short hearing. The judge handed down the sentence of ninety-three years, requiring that he serve two-thirds of the sentence without the possibility of parole because of his lack of remorse.

I realized then that the judge believed my father deserved to be punished just as much as I did. Once again it felt good to see that I wasn't alone in how I felt about my dad, and that when sane people heard what he had done, he could no longer use it as a weapon. Finally, this man could no longer hurt young children.

As I walked out of that courtroom that day, there were people who tried to get me to let them write a book about what had happened, but I just couldn't. I knew in my heart that, at that time, there was no story, just another family gone wrong, very wrong.

C hapter 15
Roller Coaster

A ROLLER COASTER IS ONLY FUN when it is mechanical, not when it's your life. As I tried to pick up the pieces and move on after the trial, my life seemed to be just that: a roller coaster of emotions.

I wanted very much to make my marriage work but I had no idea how, and I proceeded to make wrong choices and so did Chris. There were affairs on both sides, adding pain to anger and anger to pain until there really was nothing left. Still, in September of 1992, after the trial, Chris and I, vowing to save our marriage, moved to a small town in Texas with my sister Jackie, the sister I had visited and who had encouraged me to leave Skull Valley. I was so sure we could make it work. We just needed a change. I also felt that having my older sister Jackie's support was going to be such a wonderful thing I could hardly wait.

That was a time of great disillusionment in my life. I quickly learned that my sister loved my dad and "her real brothers" more than her half-sister. I tried to tell her what had happened to me as a child (she had left at seventeen, had not seen what was going on in our family, and had not been abused by my dad in anyway). She listened at first, and then one day informed me that she didn't want to hear one more thing about her dad or brothers, as she loved them very much and it hurt her too badly to hear about them.

I was devastated and crushed; I felt as if I were nothing, even though these people had done so much wrong to me. I thought I was an important sister to her, but I was terribly wrong.

We had moved into our own place by February of 1993. I worked hard to save my marriage and to care for the place that Chris and I bought, but Chris was gone day after day working for the oil company that had hired him, sometimes getting a call at 2:00 a.m. after only being home twenty-four hours or less, and then being again gone for a week or more.

I couldn't do it anymore. I was lonely, angry, and suicidal. I had never before thought of taking my life and never have again since that time. It was such a low time, and I felt trapped. Even Chris had told me, "You can never leave me; no man will ever have you; remember, you have six kids." I cried and prayed; I tried to draw close to God; I tried church; but I feared God and just knew He was mad at me and didn't truly love me. Part of me knew I was wrong; the other part feared I was right.

I was so tired of being alone. When Chris came home it was only about his needs, and then he was gone again. By the first part of June 1993, I knew I was going to leave and move back to Kingman. I didn't know how, but I knew I couldn't stay; I knew I would die. I told Chris I needed to go back to Arizona and try to figure things out. When I told my sister, she said I was crazy and shouldn't do it. I knew I had to. We had celebrated William's and Aaron's birthdays early that year so I could leave, and that's what I did.

I had been talking to an old counselor friend and I told her I really needed to go back to Arizona; I couldn't live the way I was living anymore. Her reply to me was almost too good to believe. It seems that she was running a homeless shelter out of a three-bedroom, two-bath home. She knew that she needed a break after having multiple families in the house; it had been just too tiring. She needed to have just one family there, and I fit the bill perfectly. With my six children and me in the shelter, she could just take a break. She would check in on me every few days, offering counseling and direction. It was set up; I had a home. It was a homeless shelter but it was a place to go!

As I drove away from Chris that day in June, part of me hurt very badly for my five-year-old son. He was crying, and he wanted so much to know his dad. I really hoped that I would still be able to deal with some of the pain in my chest and work our marriage out, but deep inside, I knew better; it was over for us. I knew that I would never be able to fix my marriage.

As I drove that first day, I felt something I had never known before: I felt safe, even out in the middle of nowhere. I prayed and asked God for help and knew He was with me. It was a strange time—those two days I really felt peaceful for the first time. I'm not sure why; I was a single mother with six kids, ages two through nine, driving in a 1983 Impala car with our only belongings in the world packed in the trunk of that car. I was going to live in a homeless shelter with only three hundred dollars to my name, only an eighth-grade education, and—thank you Lord—my GED.

Was I crazy? I rather thought so, but I knew I had to make changes if I was going to survive. The trip was very uneventful, but the kids had a blast. I did something that Chris had never allowed: I let the kids eat at McDonald's. I stopped at a total of four McDonald's on that trip and let them eat and play. We had so much fun.

I arrived in Kingman tired but relieved. I was home. I was with my friend the counselor, and my best friend, Ginger; I felt loved.

Once in Kingman, I looked for the address of the shelter. I found it without much trouble; there standing in the doorway was Stephanie my counselor who also ran the homeless shelter. I was so thankful to her.

The kids had nearly driven me crazy during the drive to Kingman. From the first sign that had read "Kingman 250 miles," it had been non-stop, "Are we there yet?" Now we had arrived and the kids were so excited. We looked at the house and it was perfect: beds for all of us, clean and wonderful. I felt somewhat nervous to be just given a place to live, and yet I felt a great peace that I was being cared for. We settled in rather quickly, since I really owned nothing.

I would love to say that I kept my life headed in a pure direction from that point on, but I didn't. I thank God so often, for how merciful He was to me.

I found Ginger that first day, hugged her and knew that our friendship was still very close. I was so thankful.

Before leaving to Texas, I had met Renee, who was with my old boyfriend with whom I had had the affair. She was a very young girl but seemed very nice. I had talked to her a couple of times while I was in Texas, but really didn't know her well.

However, as soon as I reached town, she tried to get me to go to a picnic in the mountains that weekend. I said yes only because I was so hungry for friendship, and I could take all the kids. The picnic was for the sheriff's department. Renee told me I would meet her dad and brother, and I said okay, not really thinking much about it.

Saturday came and to the mountains we went; there were many people there but no one I knew, so I felt kind of out of place. I was introduced to Renee's dad and brother. I was told I had met her brother before I had gone to Texas, but I only have a very vague memory of it. We talked some and he met my children. I don't really remember too much of the picnic since I was very busy with the kids. However, Renee's brother approached me and said, "Would you go to a street dance out in Chloride with me tonight? My dad lives out there; I want to go and would like it if you would come."

He was no longer just Renee's brother, he was now Rory, and he was asking me out. I should have said no, as I was still married, but instead I said, "Yes, if I can find a babysitter." I did not have or know any boundaries. So with that I set out to find a babysitter. I called my friend, Gayanne, who had given me the baby shower and asked her if her son wanted to babysit; the kids knew him and felt safe and so did I.

So, off I went, dating while still married. In my heart, I knew I would never be back with Chris, and I knew I would divorce him, but I also knew dating someone else was wrong; I did it anyway. Even though God had showed me time and time again he loved and cared for me so deeply, I could only hold onto that feeling for a very short time, as doubt and fear always crowded it out. So it became easier to try and justify my life by saying "at least I'm not as bad as my family now am I"?

We had a great time that night, and sometime around 12 o'clock, Rory took me home. I reached in to take out the items I had put in the back of his truck and when I looked up, there he was: a tall, slender, younger man. He placed a very gentle peck on my lips. I quickly hugged him, thanked him, and headed for the house.

Many days went by, and I finally asked his sister if he was still interested, or did he not like me? Well, it turned out that he thought I was mad at him for the kiss. Well, I wasn't mad; I just felt something that I really didn't want to.

Our relationship was rocky from the get–go. I truly believe it was because we were out of God's will. Had I waited until I was divorced and healed, things could have been different. Rory had many wonderful attributes that made me laugh, but he also had a very nasty temper. However it was only when he was drinking at first.

The kids grew close to him rather quickly, and he was thrilled. He really loved them and let me know that they had gotten into his heart. That was one of the reasons I wanted to remain with him, but in August of 1993, after dating only three months, he broke up with me, telling me he just wasn't sure what to do. I was devastated, but tried to keep a straight head, since I had been told that I needed to find a place to live. Stephanie was ready to start helping others again.

Even in my darkness, I was provided an apartment that fit my income. My income from the state at that time was $632 a month. I only received it one month, but it got me into the apartment:—three bedrooms and two baths—for $325 a month. I was so thankful and it came just in time; I was able to move in.

Even though Rory and I had broken up, we had many of the same friends, and when he heard I was moving, he showed up and helped. I was very grateful to see him and told him so.

Shortly after moving in, I received a phone call from the sheriff's office, advising that they were starting the processes of interviewing and testing for the correction officer job I had applied for. I was so excited. I knew it was a very hard and scary job, but I told myself that it was the only chance I had of caring for my kids, and I was not going to walk away from it. I would do everything I could to pass and become an officer. I kept telling myself that, if I could stand in a courtroom and put my father in prison, I could and would do this—this was much easier.

To complicate matters, while playing softball about four weeks earlier, I had felt a terrible tearing in my knees when I had run to first base. I hadn't warmed up and had let myself get dehydrated. I finished the bases and sat down, but when I tried to get up, I felt so much pain in my knees and legs that I could hardly stand or walk. I had no insurance, but I found twenty-five dollars to see my chiropractor, and she told me I had torn muscles. Both knees turned black and blue, swelled, and were intensely painful, but with therapy I was able to start walking again, and the bruises went away. I knew I would have to run for my correction officer test and I knew it wouldn't be easy.

I went back to my chiropractor. She had me wrap my knees in elastic bandages, and I ran, scaled the fence, overcame all the other obstacles, and passed! I was so thankful, and I thanked God.

Both knees turned black and blue and the pain was there again. But by the time I passed my background check, my knees had healed enough to start work. The background check was painful since I had to talk about why my dad was in prison. I started work the first week of October 1993. I was so thankful but I still couldn't really think about God. I was still to afraid of Him and felt that He probably didn't love me anyway.

I worked as a correction officer for almost one year; it was exhausting to have to both raise children and work. I worked three months on each shift and when graveyard shift rolled around, I wasn't sure I could handle it. That was the longest three months!

Still, that was not what ate at me every day I worked: it was the pain I saw in the eyes of many inmates, both male and female. Anger was ever-present, also. I knew my life was a mess as well, but I still felt very fortunate when I compared it to the despair in there. I could write a book just on all the sadness I saw during those twelve months. Even at that place in my life, I had a desire to find a way to help these people, mostly the women. That desire has never left me.

After the three months of graveyard shift was complete, I informed my boss I would be leaving. I knew after that year that I couldn't do it anymore. From there I would work two jobs over the next year: one as a secretary and the other as an ATM technician.

Shortly after starting my job as a correction officer, Rory came to the house one night just to see if I was doing all right and to see the kids. They were delighted to see him. He stayed for dinner, which surprised me, as he never wanted to eat with us because he "didn't want to take food out of the kids' mouths." We talked for a while, and then he was gone. Every two or three days, he would show up at the house and we would talk. He didn't say much but I knew he really still had feelings for me.

We really had some major problems. Rory was unemployed at the time but was trying to obtain work with Coca-Cola. Around the end of September, he came one night and had dinner, bringing some belongings; he told me his water had been shut off—there was a problem with the water line leading to the house he lived in, and he would have to wait for the city to repair it—and asked if he could stay until it was turned back on.

Well, that was that. He just never went home. We lived together for about three years with many ups and downs, partying, and still trying to raise kids. I was a mess, though. I was working very long hours with the ATM company and had become impossible to live with. There was a pain inside me from knowing I was not living right—whatever right was. Repeatedly, as I was drinking and dancing, this little voice would say to me, "Paula, what are you doing? I did not call you to this." It didn't matter how much fun I was having at the time, when I would hear this, I would almost immediately become sober and would ask Rory to take me home.

Our relationship started deteriorating badly after we'd been together for almost three years. The fights became worse; then he just stopped talking, went to his room, and played some kind of video game. I was so sad. In July of 1996 he just moved out. I was devastated and so were the kids. They didn't understand and missed him. I cried night and day and lost so much weight that even I was worried. Part of me just wanted to die.

Chapter 16
The Book

ONE DAY, AT A BALL GAME FOR THE KIDS, a friend of a friend said, "Hey, I have a book you need to read on forgiveness." At first I didn't want that book, remembering my own family telling me that I needed to read some book about not wasting my sorrows and that if I would have read it, I wouldn't have done the things I did like, put my dad in prison. So I was guarded at first about reading the book. Besides, what did it have to do with me? I was hurting; I didn't need to forgive, right? Wrong, and God helped me see it. After Rory left, I prayed more than I had in all my years. Something was happening in me and I wasn't sure what it was.

I finally said yes to the book and started reading it. I read it all the way through and cried and cried. I finally got it.

It was as if I heard Jesus say, "If you want My will in your life, you must surrender." It was at that moment, with tears streaming down my face, that I got down beside my bed and prayed, asking for forgiveness, and asking God to please, please, please help me to know Him, learn of Him, and understand His love and His ways.

I knew I had a new start. I felt so light inside; I felt a peace I had not felt since I first gave my life to Jesus at fourteen. I knew that I had a very long road ahead of me, but I knew I was ready. I longed to feel peace between God and me, and that day, just before my thirty-second birthday, I had a brand new start.

I wished I could say that it was all just wonderful from that day on, but when God is putting the pieces of a broken vessel back together, it's not a very easy job. I had to be patient with the healing, but fear often halted that process. Yet, my Lord and Savior have remained patient and constant through it all.

I wanted just to forget about Rory, but it was very hard to do so. I had fallen so deeply for him, and now I just had to let the Lord take care of it.

Had Rory left and never come back, it would have been easier; instead, he would call and ask to see the kids. The kids and I would sit on the floor and pray at night, and they each prayed for Rory on several occasions. I was heartbroken, so when he asked to come to their games or just come see them; it was really hard not to hope that maybe we could work things out.

I started going to a little church I had been invited to, but I felt pushed out and unworthy. Divorce was the topic most Sundays I went, and since I was divorced and had lived with a man, I didn't continue. In addition, Rory's cousin was the assistant pastor, and just seeing his cousin made me cry.

I know that my dear friend Ginger tired of my phone calls in which I'd cry and say, "I miss Rory so much," but as always, she was kind, patient, and loving. I had come to realize that I could trust her as an example of love and true friendship, and for that I will be forever thankful. God knew I needed her, and to this day, she is as a sister to me.

By September of 1996, Rory and I were not really doing any better, and his drinking was getting worse. So with a broken heart, I tried to figure out how I could just disappear and tell no one where I was.

One night Rory asked to see the kids, and I told him that I wanted to go out of town for the weekend to see my sister Ellie. I was so exhausted, and I needed a break. It was early October and I arranged to go see my sister and set up the time for Rory to get there. William was almost twelve, and I decided to leave before Rory arrived so I wouldn't have to see him. After all, all of my thinking now centered on disappearing. I couldn't take any more—I was done. As I drove to my sister's that night, I perfected the plan in my head; I knew I was done with this man.

It seems Rory decided to throw a party at my house with some of his friends. Well, I guess something happened that night. Rory says he just knew he had to see me and ask me to marry him, and to stop all the craziness. He told everyone to get out of the house, and then he asked my friend Ginger to look after the kids; this all happened very late at night. Then he proceeded to drive to my sister's house ninety miles away. He had one problem, though: he had only been there a couple of times and at night you couldn't see my sister's house, so he drove around for hours looking for me. At dawn, he finally found the house.

I was sleeping on the couch when there was a knock on the door. I was so disgusted with life that I just laid there. The knock came again, and I heard my sister get up to answer it. I laid there looking at the door, wondering who it might be. I saw the arm of the visitor and thought, oh great, this guy even has the same shirt as Rory; then I heard his voice as he asked, "Is Paula here?" My heart jumped and I got up off the couch, walked to the door, and there he stood. He asked if we could talk. I said yes, so we sat on the porch and talked, and then he told me he still loved me and wanted to get married.

Once again, I wish I could say that we married and lived happily ever after. Some may find that the only acceptable happy ending, but I have a better story—a story of redemption. I had already given my life over to the care, forgiveness and control of Jesus, but Rory had not; so begins the new story, the new beginning as the healing began.

A short time after that very memorable night, Rory and I set a wedding date: February 15, 1997. We only had a short time to get ready. I started at once and worked very hard. Money was hard to come by, but with the help of very wonderful friends, I was able to pull off a beautiful wedding. Even before the wedding, the trials would begin; we would be attacked from every angle.

First, Rory's friends told him how dumb he was and that our marriage would never work. Then a man I worked with on the ATM machines for the banks decided that he wanted to make me miserable (I later found out that he had a crush on me). Three days before my wedding, this man told his company that I had walked away from an ATM, telling him to get someone else. I was going to have my final fitting for my wedding dress, and I was so excited, but this man obviously wasn't, so he lied. Of course, I had not walked away and I had provided another technician.

The next day I was asked to meet with a woman from the Nevada branch. I did and had all my keys, pager, and phone taken on the spot. I was devastated—no explanation, just, "You no longer work for Wells Fargo ATM." I was numb; I drove home scared, sad, and angry: Why, God, why?

When I arrived home, Rory was already there, as he had received a call from his mom to say that his grandma had passed away. The grandma, who loved me as much as Rory, had hoped and prayed we would stay together and told us how she couldn't wait for our wedding. She was gone just three days before we would marry. My job was gone and now our grandma was gone, too. We laid on the floor and cried; we felt so alone, so sad and so hopeless.

I called our pastor with whom we were doing pre-marital counseling, and he agreed to meet with us. After we cried and poured out our sadness and fear, he looked at us and said, "I'm so sorry for your losses, but what I am more thankful for is that you and Rory are okay." He stated that he had feared that we would call off the wedding, and felt that that would be such a great loss, as he felt that we would do wonderful things as long as we kept our eyes on Jesus. He prayed for us and exhorted us to trust that God had a plan. I couldn't see it, and being very young in my faith, I fought to keep from crying all night. I missed grandma and was very scared about my job.

What would I do? I went through the whole process: God didn't really love me; I was really the bad one with my dad; and finally, God was there to throw me away, just as I deserved. I played this record over and over, as I had so many, many times through the years.

God had a different plan, and He simply wanted me to start the process of trusting Him, even when it looked as if all hope was gone. I received a phone call from the ATM company that had hired me in Arizona in the first place. The head of security explained to me that Nevada had jurisdiction over my job in Nevada, but they could not fire me in Arizona, so I still had a job, I would just have to help on the Arizona side. I felt such relief, and even though a part of me knew beyond anything else that God had done this, I still was too scared to believe that He had done it for me. Could He really love me?

We laid Grandma to rest on Friday and the wedding was Saturday; it was very bittersweet.

The wedding went well and was beautiful. My three oldest sons gave me away, my twin sons carried the rings, and my daughter was a flower girl along with my friend Christie's daughters. Christie had done all the flowers, my hair, and my makeup; it was so good to be the princess for one day! It was a lot of work, but worth it all. I had many wonderful friends to support me and had continued when others would have given up.

When the celebration was over we went to get in our truck, and on it in large writing was 1+1=8. It really hit home for me, as now our union did mean an instant family of eight.

We spent our wedding night in Lake Havasu in a condominium owned by my new mother-in-law. The next morning was February

16, our twin's seventh birthday, so it was off to the store to buy gifts and head back for their party.

Then on Monday, we left on a very wonderful trip to Maui for one week. What a wonderful time! So many people helped make it possible, and it was a much needed time for Rory and me. We hadn't been alone for any length of time since it was very hard to find people willing to help with our clan. However, the daughter of my counselor offered to care for the kids while we were gone. I'm sure she will never know what that meant to Rory and me, never! I was humbled and blessed beyond words. These were more of the times that helped me to see how God loved me and wanted to care for me.

Marriage would prove a challenge for us from the get–go; so many issues: bills, children, job problems, and Rory's drinking— sometimes quite a lot—made life hard. I started spending much time praying and asking God to help me know how to be a good wife and mother. I was still so afraid of God and felt as if He might just let me go at any time, but still I prayed, believing even though I really didn't see.

Because I had lost the position in Laughlin, Nevada just before my wedding, it didn't mean I didn't have a job; however, it was hard for the company to find work for me in Arizona, as all the positions in Kingman were full. I did still ride with my dear friend Ginger to receive a paycheck, but it was very scary—I really was not needed in the area.

As spring arrived, Rory and I started talking about moving. We didn't really know where we wanted to go, we just wanted to go. We needed a fresh start; we needed green: What about Texas, what about this place and that? But we had no real answers, just a desire to move.

One night in April, Rory called and said, "Hey, Jim is coming into town tonight. Let's go out," I felt sick to my stomach, as this could only mean one thing: drinking, and lots of it. We met at a bar/

restaurant, and the shots started before the meal. Very little of the meal was eaten by Rory or Jim.

I drank just enough to keep Rory from getting mad. I pretended to be drinking but just sipped very slowly. I knew I had to stay sober; besides, the Holy Spirit was with me and I didn't want to be drunk. We left and went to a bar, and there, as usual, things went from bad to worse. Jim got out of line with an ex-girlfriend, and I became angry dealing with drunks. We had to get Jim out before the police arrived, and Rory became quite angry with me.

We dropped Jim off at his motel and went home. However, I was angry by then and tried to reason with Rory about how he had treated me: *bad mistake!* Soon there was a full fight and Rory, drunk, decided he was leaving. I called 911 and the police came very quickly. I felt my life was over: I was surrounded by glass from a broken window, and my new husband telling the police, as they cuffed him and took him away, that he wanted a divorce.

That played through my mind the rest of the night as I lay on the couch, shaking and crying, "It's over, it's over. What good could ever come from this, God?" I still remember asking God that very question and feeling so much fear and sadness. I didn't know it then, but there would be a silver lining to a very dark situation; God was starting to work!

Not that sleep came that night, because it didn't; but morning still came. I'm not sure when I called my mother-in-law, but I did, and then I found out what time Rory would go to court. Rory's mom was very upset but was still kind to me. It was very hard for her because he was her son.

We arrived just in time to see Rory being taken to the courthouse, chain gang style. Since he had been wearing cowboy boots, considered a weapon, he had to walk in his socks. I will never forget the guilt and fear that I felt, I could only remember the words, "I want a divorce," from him the night before.

There was no eye contact and he avoided me as best he could. I felt sick. I prayed and prayed, asking Jesus to please help Rory and me. He was released, but his family was heartbroken and humiliated. It was a very hard time for us, but the real changes were in Rory. Even though his external self didn't show it much, inside he had made a commitment to change, that also included starting to believe that God was real, that Jesus did love him, and that he needed forgiveness.

Chapter 17
New Start, New Home

THE DESIRE TO LEAVE KINGMAN and make a new start was overpowering. Rory and I began to pray about it daily. I was still trying to sell the property that had been awarded to me through my divorce. The property was rented out and time and time again, over a three year period, our renters had tried to get a loan to buy the property. I would get my hopes up, only for them to be dashed. My hopes were that we could get the money so that we could move, but nothing happened.

In my prayers I often still felt as if God really did not hear me or care. That was nothing new for me; it was my life, even though I had started to realize that there were times it seemed God did hear and did love me.

I continued to pray for guidance in our move, half believing, and half doubting that He heard me. Then one day my friend Ginger said to me, kind of half heartedly, "so you wouldn't be interested in moving to Payson, Arizona, would you?" It seemed that the ATM company we worked for needed someone in Payson.

It didn't take much thinking. I remembered in the back of my mind that this was a little town in the mountains in central Arizona. It had been years since I had been there, but I started to feel an excitement. I told her I would love to check it out.

I called the ATM company, and after telling my boss that I wanted to try it out, he said that he needed me to go to Payson the next weekend to give the man that worked there a weekend off. The company would pay for everything. I was very excited as I tried to tell my husband, who by now was very cautiously excited, that this might be the place to go.

Rory got off work on Friday and after securing a babysitter, we left for Payson. It was very late when we arrived, but the monsoon rains had already started. It was late June and it was beautiful. We had a wonderful weekend and after talking about it, felt it was okay to tell the company we would like to consider the position. I was still very nervous. We had not sold the property in Kingman and we really had no money, so even though I told the company I wanted to consider it, I asked just to work there every other weekend for a spell until we could figure it out.

A couple of weekends later we went back, this time with all the kids. They had a wonderful time, but they wanted me to know that they were not happy about moving; they wanted to stay in Kingman forever! I was concerned. I really didn't know where we would live or how we could do this, and now the kids were angry. I was scared. Did God really want this, and how would we do it? We had no extra money. God, what could we do? We needed help!

The first of July came and we were sure that we wanted to move, but still kept thinking, how? Then Rory came home and announced, out of the blue, that his last day at work was the last of July and that he was moving to Payson to live and find work. Jobs were scarce, very scarce and I panicked: he had not even asked me! I was so scared! What would happen? I prayed in desperation: God, Lord Jesus, please help us.

I had heard a rumor that our renters were going to attempt to get the money to finally buy the property we were trying to sell. I refused to get excited—I had too many times before—but I finally prayed and said, "God, you see our need, and if this move is your will, please provide."

Day by day, as the month of July wore on, I felt more panicked; there still were no funds even for Rory to leave his job and go. But deep inside I felt a small peace that God was in control. I was having a kind of last lunch together with some friends at the bowling alley when my pager went off. As I looked at the number, I realized it was my renter, so I went to a pay phone and called her. It was just days before Rory's job was over, so when I heard Sandy say, "Your money is at the title company, you can get it whenever you want," I knew that God was in total control and it was meant that we should go. I called Rory and told him. We were so excited and grateful.

Deciding to go and actually going were definitely two separate things. We put our house on the market and Rory moved to Payson. He lived first in a motel and then, when we bought a camp trailer, he moved into a trailer park. That was much better.

Rory went out many days with real estate people looking for a place, but to no avail. We prayed and prayed: Lord, where is the right place to be? Help us.

I went to Payson for my job one weekend in July, and during that time, we had an agent show us many places. There was one we could afford but someone else beat us to it, so after much frustration, the man said to us that he knew of a place that wasn't even finished yet. It was on one acre—one of the requirements we had since I felt the kids needed room to play. After looking at the place, we knew that if it were possible, we wanted it. It was the right price. It was directly across from the RV park in which Rory was staying. The home itself was a mobile home. It was old, filthy, and needed much work. It was also a very small, with only three bedrooms and two baths. It was definitely no dream, but it was what we could afford, so we said yes and bought it as an owner carry.

With the money from our place in Kingman, we paid off all debt and put $15,000 down on the new place. We were broke but we had a home, and if I worked hard enough I would make it a nice place; it would be fine and I was so happy!

We moved, scared and excited, to Payson on Labor Day weekend 1997. We started getting the house ready and the gas and electric turned on; we had a well for water.

All seemed fine until the gas company arrived and said that the stove and water heater could not be lit because they were unsafe. I looked at them I realized they were really in bad shape. The refrigerator was awful, too, and smelled of mold; I couldn't get the smell out. The dishwasher was not good either. I felt sick. So, $4,000 later, all on credit cards, we were again in debt but had a functioning home.

With lots of elbow grease, I was able to clean the grease off of all the cabinets, and painting them made the kitchen look much better. I had to wash down all the walls, which had thick black smoke on them, but I was thankful.

We loved the town and the people seemed nice. Rory got a job at a fencing company: Wow, what a tough job! He really worked hard, but it was a job, and I had my job, so we tried to settle in.

We were making payments on the Kingman house as well as the Payson house and it was very tough. Winter was coming and in the back of my mind, there was this little reminder that in March of the coming year we would need to come up with a $10,000 balloon payment or refinance the house. I tried not to worry about it, as there was plenty to do, with six kids, all in school now, and my job.

Rory's court hearing for the domestic violence in Kingman was finally over, and he was ordered to twelve months of AA and then anger management classes. It was hard for him attend those, just because he was so tired, but he never missed one.

The cold set in and we realized that our home was very, very hard to heat. With a fireplace and central heat, we were paying huge bills for gas and were still cold. It was tough.

Then Rory came home one day in November just before Thanksgiving and said he had been laid off. Wow, was that ever painful. Fear gripped me. What would we do? Two mortgages, one income, and six children. I felt sick.

I called the real estate agency in Kingman and begged them to let the house go for what we owed, and with God's grace and mercy, a couple weeks later it did sell for what we owed. I was sad not to make anything, but it was good to have only one mortgage. Rory needed a job badly, but there just were not any available. He tried with the schools, but with his court issues, he couldn't work for the school system.

Then he started the court-ordered anger management classes. He met a man who would give him his first job with a special type of drying system. But the job would not start until February, and he needed six months on the job to get a loan for the house. The balloon payment was due in March.

It all seemed so impossible, but I started trying for a loan in March. I soon found out that there were obstacles that were much bigger than even I knew in the beginning. I found out that the mobile home we had bought was pre-HUD. I didn't even know what that meant but I soon found out: that it meant that it would be impossible to find a loan.

I called more places, pleading my case as the fear mounted in my chest every day. I truly didn't know what to do or say. We had started going to church regularly but I was too scared to say anything to any of the people.

I cried and prayed, asking God to help us. It was April now and the owners informed me they had started repossession papers. I was so angry and scared. Then one day I was told to go see a man who was the "best in town." Half-heartedly but still hoping, I walked in his office and explained my very large problem: that I needed a loan on a pre-HUD mobile, that the owners were already starting repossession, and that my husband had just started a new job. I spilled it out and my frustration and fear were evident.

Glen looked at me and said, "Well, I think I can help you." Those were the most beautiful words I had heard in along time. He also said, "I know the owner and I will call him and ask him to be patient." Then the tears started. I just knew this man was going to help, I could feel it and I just couldn't stop the tears.

It took work. I had to come up with more paperwork than one could imagine, but a few weeks later we had a loan. The relief was so great, and my heart was so thankful. I knew that God had seen us through, and I made an altar in my mind that I visit when Satan attacks and I remind myself how my Lord and Savior met me and heard my prayers.

This was truly the first test I had gone through; were there was no doubt that God was showing me, even though it was through hardship, how much He loved me, and wanted to care for me.

After the loan went through the relief was wonderful; however, we still owned a pre-HUD mobile that, if you looked closely at it, was a real piece of junk: holes in the floor; ceiling falling in, among other things; a leaky roof, no matter how hard we tried to fix it. When the wind blew, the curtains moved; but for the time being, it was a time of celebration, praise, and joy! I felt so much relief, and the realization that Jesus loved me was so real, more so than at any other time of my life. I was truly aware of His love so close to me. I reflect on it when times are tough even today.

The kids were growing so fast, and the church we were going to was a great support in helping them know who Jesus was. My own distorted view of my Lord and Savior was one of so much fear and legality that it often brought out a very legal view of God instead of love. It hurts me to think of it now, but it was all I knew.

All my children were baptized as they gave their hearts to Jesus, and those were very wonderful times for me. Rory and I continued to grow also. There was so much damage done to me that the process was very slow, but with many loving brothers and sisters in Christ, the healing and spiritual growth was truly starting.

Rory's job was going quite well and the mobile home was getting worse. Many areas of the floor were falling through, and the only thing that kept that from really happening was the carpet over those areas; we tried to walk on the two-by-fours as much as possible.

I started the process of buying a new custom- built prefab home. I prayed and prayed for guidance, and the Lord was very good in guiding me to the best deal one could find: a wonderful five-bedroom, three-bath, built just for us.

The process took quite a long time, about six months all together, but what fascinated me was how I was recognizing the hand of my Lord.

Rory had to work in another state during this time and only came home on the weekends, if he could, so the whole process was left up to me.

I was desperate to have a home, so I worked my two jobs, took care of the six children and fought the battles of removing the old home from, and having a new one put on, the property.

God blessed me with people who were honest. However, when it came time to level the lot, one was not; but the owner of the excavation company made him do the job properly, for no charge. When the home was delivered, the towing tongues were on the wrong end, even though I had requested otherwise. Nevertheless, I was provided with people and a tractor to help to put it into place, and I got a refund.

When I ordered the house, I had it come untapped and without texture to save money. Once it was joined together, friends volunteered to tape and texture the whole inside of the house. I was so humbled. Then the house needed painting, and a wonderful family I hardly knew painted the whole house. Another man donated the paint and plaster for the tape and texture. The family that painted became our family later, when my eldest son, William, fell in love with their lovely daughter, Shelly, and they married.

Then there was the issue of all the electric, gas, and water lines, and all the inspections that had to be passed. Randy, the worship leader at our church, arrived as early as five o'clock every morning and worked until it was too hot for him. Most of the people that helped were from our church, loving me/us into understanding the love of God.

From the time we had to move out of our old mobile home until the time we could move into the new one, seven weeks passed. Where do you put six kids? Well, God provided loving homes. Randy and Kathy took the twins and their son enjoyed having their company, and then Joe, who had become related to us when his son married Shelly's sister, took my three oldest sons. Joe's children were sort of "my kids" since his wife had left and they lived very close, so I was glad to have them at my home. Joe was also the first one to invite us to the church we now belonged to. My daughter and I stayed in a motor home my neighbor let us borrow.

The reason I tell all of this is to paint a picture of the family that God started providing for me.

While I was dealing with all these circumstances, often fear would try to creep in, and it sometimes planted its feet quite well, especially when my husband called one night to tell me that he wasn't sure if the job was going to last much longer. I was petrified. We had to close on this loan, but unless he had this job, we couldn't. That happened at the first part of May, just as we had pulled the old mobile home off the property, so for seven weeks I cried out to the Lord to help us and He did. We signed the papers just one week before the job ended.

I felt so humbled by the whole experience. The children were so happy to have a warm place in the winter, no bugs coming up through the floor, five brand new bedrooms, and three bathrooms. What a blessing! It cost extra for that third bathroom and we couldn't have it added without the help of my mother-in-law who has always been a loving, kind and encouraging part of our lives. Finally, I was living in a place out of which I did not have to scrub other people's filth. I cried tears of joy and smiled a lot as we settled in.

God knows when we can take no more and since I was dealing with the problems of putting the new home on the property and all it included, I would have never been able to hear that Rory's job was ending with no other insight! We still had to close on the loan while he was at his job, but we also needed to be able to pay that loan! So God brought about a job for Rory that he found out about just before the other one ended and this one was in the same field, just much better pay, a much better boss (a wonderful Christian man) and he started just days after the other one ended.

We settled into our new home and into having a full time husband and dad again. It wasn't easy, in a way, as there was always adjusting to do. However, love won through, and I enjoyed the time raising my children, watching many baseball games and seeing the boys grow into young men and my daughter grow into a wonderful young girl.

My heart was overjoyed at times and overwhelmed at others. I knew something that no one else truly understood. My children were growing up in a good home: not perfect, but good. I felt so much strength and joy over the feeling that it helped me through the times when I had so little money to stretch that I was exhausted. Working two jobs at all times and throwing a third one in as needed, I often had a hard time coming home and cooking meals. I did, however, and those are some of my best memories.

Being pushed to perform at such a high rate constantly took a toll on my health and I was often in pain. In 1999, I started getting lumps on my legs that were very painful. I finally went to a doctor and was told they were "just bug bites." Later in 2003 after a biopsy, I was told I had a very serious disease and then later told I had a less serious one that I live with today; it is serious but not as serious as the first diagnosis. I have an autoimmune disease, but with careful eating and proper nutrition, it is well controlled.

Chapter 18
A New Blessing

THE YEAR 2000 WAS FAST APPROACHING, and there was quite a stir. People were scared. What do we do? The world is ending. Should we store food? Fear was everywhere. People moved from large cities and two of those people were a grandmother and granddaughter. They had moved in across from us in the RV Park. I had not met the granddaughter, but my youngest daughter had, and she had made friends with her. Marie was eight, and having a young girl around was great for her.

Often Marie told me of her loneliness; she was the only girl and the youngest, with five older brothers. I felt sad for her, and Rory and I had even prayed about adopting, but we were unsure whether that was a good idea or not.

Well, when God has a plan, He just makes it work. Marie had prayed for a sister, and Rory and I had prayed for God's will on the issue. I remember Marie telling me that her little friend, Alexandra, didn't have a mom and that she lived with her grandmother. It was not a good situation for either Alexandra or the grandmother. Marie and Alexandra became quite the friends. Marie even led Alexandra to give her heart to Jesus while sitting on the trampoline.

Not long after I met Alexandra and her grandmother, her grandmother needed to leave town to train for a new job and asked if we would watch Alexandra for the week. I was dumbfounded, as I did not feel she knew us well enough to leave her with us, but she did, and I felt that at least with us, I knew she was safe.

Something happened in my heart that week. That little girl seemed so lost and alone it hurt me. There were signs that the grandmother was not handling the responsibility of her granddaughter, and it stressed me out greatly. However, I felt I couldn't do much.

About a month later, the grandmother moved into the town of Payson (we lived 4 miles out of the town of Payson), so I didn't hear too much about "Allie" for a while. I felt an ache for her every time I asked Marie. She told me what she knew: that her grandmother had given Allie to a family, and that she seemed very lost.

Then one day, Allie's grandmother called me and started telling me all her issues with Allie. She felt Allie was more than she could handle. She was afraid that she might do something to hurt her, so she was giving her to CPS (child protective services). I wasn't sure what to think. I started praying immediately, asking for guidance; the thought of the little girl going into the foster care system was more than I could bear.

I called Rory and told him what was going on, and he said, without hesitation, "You need to get her. Start making calls and see what you can do." I started by calling CPS. I found out that if I could get the grandmother to sign a power of attorney to give Allie to me, then she could be "spared the system"! I called the grandmother; she readily agreed, and in front of CPS, she signed the paperwork. Two days after Allie's eighth birthday, Allie came to live with us permanently.

There were many tough times, but ultimately, what a blessing and joy it was to raise Allie. We had passed the background check, so she could stay with us. We felt blessed and so did Marie: she had her sister and she was thrilled.

Now, raising seven children had many challenges—providing for them and still having time for each one was often very trying. I often still fought each and every day with fear about whether God would provide. There always seemed to be challenges. I questioned every day how it was all going to work. I was still fighting with the fear that God might still just drop me off and let me die. However, it helped so much to be able to reflect on the times that my God had brought me through what seemed impossible situations. I knew that healing was happening as time went on, and the times of extreme fear became fewer. I started to realize that I had a Father who truly loved me.

Chapter 19
Do You Trust Me?

JUNE OF 2004 SEEMED A GOOD TIME. We had made it through having another child join our home, as well as the bombing of the twin towers, better known as 9/11. My daycare was doing well, and our oldest son, William, was planning to marry. I was very excited about the wedding, as I knew he was marrying a wonderful girl who is now a wonderful wife, mother, and daughter-in-law.

Several of the kids had had surgeries at the beginning of the year, but none was serious; however, it was painful to see my kids go through them, and tiring and trying for me. I still was very tired most of the time, but daily naps with the daycare kids—when they would nap—helped to some degree. As June of 2004 rolled around, the diagnosis of an autoimmune disease for me seemed well under control and I started to relax.

On June 4, 2004, one of our friend Joe's sons was getting married; of course, we were excited about the wedding. It took place on a Saturday morning. Our youngest daughter, Allie, was going to Florida on Sunday for a visit, and I found it a perfect time to see my cousin, so we attended with plans that I leave after the wedding to go to Phoenix. I kissed my husband, and off I went with my two girls.

It was a special weekend because I had never just taken the girls and spent time with them; I was very excited. We had a great time, did some shopping and all the fun stuff. On Sunday morning, I knew we had to be at the airport early, so I said goodbye to my cousin and off we went. I had plans to do more shopping with Marie after we put Allie on the plane.

We arrived at the airport, but had some problems with Allie's flight and needed information from home. I was worried because I thought that Rory and the other kids would already be in church. I called anyway, and to my surprise, Rory answered the phone. I asked for the information and then asked, "Why are you still home?" I will never forget his answer: "Well, I have some double vision in my eyes." It was as if I had been hit in the stomach. I sensed it was bad, but when I said that he needed to go to a doctor right away, his reply was, "I just need to see an eye doctor." Well, I knew better, but right then was not the time to say anything, so I told him I loved him and then, in a fog, I put Allie on the plane. I no longer felt like shopping. I told Marie I was sorry, and with her understanding, we went home.

The sick spot in my stomach was still there when I arrived home. There sat my husband in his chair. I asked, "How do you feel?" He said, "Just tired, very tired. I just need sleep."

I fought with him for several hours about going to the hospital, but he kept refusing. Finally, a friend and neighbor, who we picked on much of the time because she talked so much, told me, "I'm coming over." When she arrived, she told Rory that she was going to continue talking until he went to the hospital. It was amazing—he became instantly willing!

The emergency room personnel weren't sure what to make of the situation. By then, he was weak and having a hard time keeping one eye open, and the double vision was worse. A CAT scan was done, but it showed nothing, and he was sent home with some medicine for an inner ear infection.

By Monday, he was worse, with extreme fatigue, double vision, and eyes that now both wanted to close. I called our family doctor who had been in the ER the night before, and his reply was, "Just give the medicine some time to work."

By Tuesday morning, Rory couldn't walk. He could only crawl. I knew I had to do something, so I started looking into taking him to Barrows Neurological Institute at St. Joseph's Hospital in Phoenix, about eighty miles away. I was looking for the phone number when Rory's boss called and said, "Paula could you get Rory to St Joseph's in Phoenix?" I knew then that I had confirmation as to where we needed to go. Jim, his boss, had the number and address. I called and was told to get him there as soon as possible.

With great effort, we got him in the van, and I drove. I was feeling so much fear—I was so afraid he might die on me. His head was bent down, and he had no strength to hold it up. I know I drove too fast, but I just couldn't help feeling he might die on me.

We arrived at the hospital and sat in the emergency room for almost four hours. It was very frustrating, but as ambulances came in with patients with heart problems and from car accidents, we just had to sit and wait.

Just a short time before we were called in, Rory's mom and stepdad arrived. It was so good not to be alone. The pain in his mom's eyes when she saw Rory was heart breaking. We all fought back tears. Finally, we were called in, and the testing began: spinal tap, MRIs, CAT scans, blood work and questioning. We were exhausted.

Sometime during the late night my sister Ellie and her husband came. The comfort, love, and her sense of humor, which Rory understood and enjoyed so much, were a great help.

I'm not sure when I finally left with my mother-in-law to get some sleep, but I can tell you it was a waste of time. I couldn't sleep, and the one time I dozed off, I woke with so much fear I couldn't breathe. I once again felt that maybe, just maybe, God was angry with me, and now it was all going to fall apart. I prayed, but mostly just said, "Please God, please; I'm so scared." Then came the feeling of fear that I was not going to make it through this, that Rory would die and I would be alone raising our kids.

My son's wedding was to be July 31: what if he missed it? One moment I would feel that God was with me, the next I felt alone. Our church was praying and I prayed, but could God actually take us through this? He had done so much for me, but what about this? What was wrong with my husband?

The next morning when I arrived at the hospital, I found out that he finally had a room. As I made my way to his room with his mom, I felt as if I were in a bad dream. I entered his room and there he lay; he looked so small and weak. He was very cold to the touch and very, very weak. He started talking, so I put my ear up to his mouth and he said very weakly, "I do love you so much, but I'm not sure I'm going to make it. I'm forgetting to breathe, and it's hard to breathe." I knew at that moment I had to do something.

I walked out of that room and walked to the nurses' station. It didn't take long to get someone's attention. I asked why we didn't know anything yet, and where was the doctor? "Please, what is wrong with my husband?" It was then that I was told that he had been diagnosed and that medication was on its way. I explained that he couldn't breathe and couldn't even remember to breathe.

The response was quick, then, and in a very short time, a doctor was there, explaining both what was wrong and what medication was needed. The very foreign words, *myasthenia gravis,* came from that doctor's mouth. I had no more of an idea of the problem after being told what was wrong than I had had before being told. It was all such a foreign world.

Over time, we would learn that it was an autoimmune problem that affected the neurotransmitters, which made his muscles fail. He was in what was called "crisis." After receiving the first medications, he seemed to get better within hours. I was very excited; I thought he would just take meds and go back to work the following Monday!

I was wrong, though, and he proceeded to get much worse before getting better. It was a very trying time. Within a couple of weeks, Rory started falling. Actually, his first fall was on his thirty-fifth birthday, when he became so weak he couldn't even get out of bed.

Once again, the fear set in: was God punishing me? Was He going to let Rory die? I couldn't fathom the thought, yet as I looked at him and read about his disease and listened to people I knew, I realized it could happen. The real possibility was there that Rory might never work or walk again. We still had five children at home. I worked very hard to put on a strong face for Rory, but would go to the steps at the end of our house, sit there, cry, pray, and try to figure out what to do. Really, there was not much I could do except wait on the Lord.

When I brought Rory home from the hospital, I was still running my Department of Economic Security Daycare out of my home. So now, I had to care for Rory, along with all the day-to-day workings of our home with our children and the day care. I was so sick at heart it was hard to put one foot in front of the other, let alone take care of all the rest. The hardest part was stopping the belief that I deserved this and that God was mad at me. I prayed so much, and all our church family prayed for us. I came to feel a peace in my heart that my Lord and Savior, who loved me and Rory and our children, was allowing a test, and that He was with us, as He always has been and always will.

Our oldest son's wedding was on July 31. Rory's whole goal was to be able to walk by then and he was, although only for short periods; still, we were very thankful. What a wonderful wedding!—an occasion of joy for our son and his new wife, but also for Rory's obvious healing.

Rory and I learned a great deal through the illness, and praise God every time the realization comes to us that he could have died, Instead, seven years later, God has brought healing, and Rory has been in remission for four years now.

We will be forever grateful to Rory's boss, Jim. While Rory was so ill that he could not go to work, Jim continued to see to it that Rory received full, pay as well as insurance and supplements that truly helped Rory. We give God the glory and thank his boss for being the tool that God could use. We know we were blessed.

While running the daycare was great for a season, I knew that I could not continue for long, so starting shortly before Rory's illness, I worked to get my Medical Billing Certificate. It was very challenging, but my goal was to have a job from home that actually paid me.

However, God had other plans. I realized that I would need to work in an office first, and God provided me with my first job in an orthopedic doctor's office. That job didn't turn out as I had hoped; the office was severely mismanaged.

I started to feel as if I wouldn't be able to find a job that was worth it, but then a new doctor came to town. A very wonderful friend who went to our church and worked at the hospital recommended me for the position of office manager/medical biller. I was thrilled, but scared to death. When I met the doctor, he hired me on the spot! Wow! How good God was.

Finally, after all these years, I would have a good job, one in which I could make a good living; and coupled with my husband's salary, we could pay our bills, help our kids, and have a little extra. Finally, it was all coming together. I made plans in my head for the future; I was really thinking that I had arrived at a pretty good spot. My job started in October of 2006, and the office opened in November. I had helped open a doctor's office and it was brand new: a new doctor, new office, and new job. I wasn't at home, but I didn't care; I was having a great time.

I felt all was going well and would just get better; I had waited for so long. I had a clear view of where my life would to go: I would work for this doctor for many years, if not until retirement; Rory enjoyed his job and had 61/2 years in with a great Christian boss/owner who really cared for us. It was perfect, finally!

"We make plans and God laughs," I heard it said many times, and I would soon learn the true meaning of that.

God wasn't finished with me yet, and since I regularly gave my will over to Him, I should not have been surprised when I received a call just three months after I started my new job and just about one month after having the feeling that I had "arrived." It was my husband, telling me that he could no longer handle working with the new man who had been put in charge of his company and that he had quit. I was shocked, but because he had done this once before and had decided to stay, I felt a little hope that he would work it out with his company. I was wrong; he was very sure and even though his boss expressed that he wanted him to stay, the answer was set in stone: he was done with that company. I was devastated, crushed, felt helpless and oh so angry. How could he do this?

We went to counseling with our pastor, my anger, mixed with tears, flowing out of me. I was so angry that I really considered leaving. I wanted my security! I wanted my dream! I wanted the life for which I felt I had worked so hard! I also believed that, since my husband had left his job, somehow I had a right to be angry! I had a meltdown, and tears and anger consumed me.

I could see that my husband was sad for me, but he seemed happier than ever as he tried for a new job here, there and everywhere. My anger and now fear ran so deep that counseling with our pastor and his wife was a must. Even though they understood my circumstances, I was encouraged to seek God and let Him guide me through this.

When I sought God, "trust me" was his answer, and that was so very hard do. Even as I write this, a new level of understanding comes to me that my Lord and Savior Jesus Christ wanted me to trust Him and Him alone. Yes, there were issues in my husband's life that God wanted to work on, but never believe a trial is just for one spouse: it's always two-edged.

For me, because of my past, trust has been my number one failure and God's number one requirement. One may say, and I have also said, "but I have such a reason to fail in the area of trust," and yes, I do, but if I want God's best for me, *I must trust Him and Him alone!*

The anger and rebellion I felt in my heart over my husband leaving his job stayed, though. I resided with my emotions every day as my husband went from one idea or job to another. None was enough to meet our financial needs, and each time I justified my anger toward him by citing all the issues.

By June of 2006, I had come to the end of my resources; I gave myself over to my Lord. The relief was wonderful, and in July, God answered our prayers for a job for my husband. At first, I was so excited, but then anger set in as I realized once again our whole life was going to be turned upside down.

The job was two hundred miles away in a little town south of Tucson, Arizona. This would mean our four youngest children would have to leave the school and friends that they had known for so long; they were in their high school years. I just can't do it—I told myself—it's so wrong. My kids were angry too, especially my twins, who were in their junior year and very shy.

Rory accepted the position in July of 2006. I decided to stay in Payson for many reasons; reasons for which I felt completely justified: my job, the kids's school, my new grandbaby, and of course the fact that Rory had made his choice. I wasn't even sure he would stay with the job. I felt justified in refusing every time that still small voice called the Holy Spirit said to me, "Paula, you belong with your husband." I argued that I needed to stay for this or that reason; besides, he came home every weekend, or I went to him, and at first, it seemed kind of nice.

God had a plan, and even though I was putting up a fight, I had given my life to Him many years before. In His love and kindness, my heavenly Father sent a very special person through a very special friend of mine to share God's will in a way that made me realize there was no mistake. I had to go to my husband.

I enjoy telling this story because of the power and beauty with which God does things.

I walked the park in Payson several times a week and said good morning to a very pleasant woman who just seemed to be so happy. She walked with gusto, and she was there several times while I was. I had no idea who she was.

I received a phone call one day during this time from my dear friend, Gayanne, who had been such a support to me through the years. She told me that her friend, Judy, was living in Payson at this time, and that she was working at a local church; Gayanne wanted us to meet. I was so excited to meet her friend who, according to Gayanne, loved the Lord and was a wonderful person. So we decided to meet at the local coffee shop.

I walked in that day, expecting to see an elderly woman with kind of a saintly look, maybe with gray hair: you know, the way we tend to think of "Godly" people, but instead there was that little dynamite lady from the park!—Not even five feet tall, with fiery dark eyes, dark hair, and a contagious smile. I introduced myself as Gayanne's friend and so did she.

A very special friend had brought us together, and now God was going to work. I sat down and we exchanged a few introductory pleasantries, and then Judy took my hand and said to me, "I realize I hardly know you, but God has told me to tell you this. I hope you will receive it. God wants you to be with your husband." The tears started flowing, and as my heart started to thaw, I felt love, real love. I agreed with Judy and right there we prayed.

I could not tell you the rest of our conversation that day, but our purpose for meeting had been accomplished! God had used both women to get the message to me of His will and his love. It's not that I didn't know it already, because I did, but I was too angry to act on it, and too afraid to believe that God had any other plan. What a mistake! It took time to move to be with my husband, but with a willing heart, God made it all possible.

But there are always consequences to rebellion, and by not putting our house on the market in 2006, I had missed the opportunity to sell our home while the market was still good. By the time I did put it on the market, the market was crumbling, and four years later, it still has not sold. However, God has been merciful and has provided good renters.

There have been many doors opened in my new home, and God has worked out to His glory many of the situations that have seemed impossible.

I continue to be challenged in the area of trust more than anywhere else. I feel that anytime I think I have arrived, God allows a new challenge, as He grows me with His tender love to become the child He has called me to be. Through all the hard times, all the abuse, and all the sin, I can learn of the mercies of my Savior, the One who is there and has always been there since before I was even born.

Chapter 20
A New Family

ONE OF THE BLESSINGS THAT GOD HAS GIVEN ME through all this was the unfailing love of Suzann. When I was pregnant with my twins and she was only 49, she suffered a stroke it was very debilitating to her speech but just as soon as she could talk, even though it was hard to understand her we started to talk on a regular basis.

I even was able to see her after I moved to Texas, since she was living there at that time also. Suzann was faithful in letting me know she loved me, but it was very hard for her to understand that I really had a hard time trusting! She confronted me one day and said, "You can try to get away from me if you like, but I'm not going to leave you." I realized I was too scared to let her love me. Over time, trust grew. She became my "Mom" and I her "daughter"; she loves my children and is a wonderful grandma. Grandma Suzy is loved, and so is Grandpa Larry, her husband.

But it wasn't enough for her; she wanted to be my mother legally, and "Pa" Larry wanted to be my legal father. In the midst of Rory leaving his job and all the turmoil, I was legally adopted at the age of forty-two. It was a surreal feeling. I have fully accepted it now and have had a dose of taking care of parents last year when my Pa was diagnosed with multiple myeloma. It makes me feel like I truly am their daughter! Pa is doing well at this point, and we all continue to hope and pray.

Chapter 21
Today

AS I FINISH PUTTING MY LIFE ON PAPER, I include very little about my children since keeping their privacy has been important to me. But I want it known that my children were my number one inspiration to get up and keep going, each and every day. I worked very hard not to let my past affect our home life. I also spoke very little to my children about the abuse until it was very age appropriate.

I wanted so badly to have my children know home-cooked meals, a clean home. I wanted them to feel that I loved them and know that they were safe. I'm sure I was not perfect, but just to hear my children say as grownups that it is hard to understand how a child can be abused is enough for me.

They are a great inspiration even today. All have moved out as of May, 2010, and at times the loneliness is hard, but the joy makes it worth it as I reflect on each of my children. I am thankful that they helped me walk this road to recovery, each and every one—even the new ones (daughter-in-laws) and grandchildren. All continue to bring healing and joy as I realize how good God is. It was very important for each of my children to complete high school, and each one has. Some have almost finished college, and others are working hard to get there. God has given me family and love. I pray that our family can continue to grow in the love, knowledge, and holiness of our Savior. Thank you, my children, for your love and support.

I'm learning that I will never "arrive" while on this earth. There is always going to be changes: some wonderful, some hard, and some tragic. There will be trials and tribulation as long as I'm here.

However, I know now that my Savior has seen every single tear I have cried, and that he is continuing to grow and heal me. In turn, I pray that every person who reads this book will realize that no matter how seemingly big or small your pain or issue, the Lord Jesus is there for each and every one. Not just me or someone else. He is there for you; yes, you!

If you will commit your life to the Savior and ask Him to forgive your sins and to help you on the road to discovering Him, He will faithfully do so, and along the way you will discover a Savior, a friend, and a Father, and healing—beautiful sweet healing!

CPSIA information can be obtained at www.ICGtesting.com
Printed in the USA
LVOW060749250613

340018LV00001B/9/P